# *Going Places* with Youth Outreach

## Smart Marketing Strategies for Your Library

## ANGELA B. PFEIL

AMERICAN
LIBRARY
ASSOCIATION

Chicago

2005

**PERMISSIONS**

Figure 2.1 is used with permission of the Las Vegas–Clark County Library District.

Figure 2.2 is used with permission of the Hennepin County Library District.

Figure 2.3 is used with permission of the Las Vegas–Clark County Library District.

Card images (figures 2.4 and 2.5) are used with permission of the Las Vegas–Clark County Library District.

Card image (figure 2.6) is used with permission of the Henderson District Public Libraries.

Card image (figure 2.7) is used with permission of the Hennepin County Library District.

Card images (figures 2.8 and 2.9) are used with permission of the King County Library System.

Figure 2.10 is used with permission of the Multnomah County Library District.

Figure 5.4 is used with permission of the Las Vegas–Clark County Library District.

Screen shot (figure 7.1) is used with permission of the Multnomah County Library District.

Box 8.1 is used with permission of the Las Vegas–Clark County Library District.

Box 8.2 is used with permission of the Multnomah County Library District.

Figure 8.1 is used with permission of the Hennepin County Library District.

---

Printed on 50-pound white offset, a pH-neutral stock, and bound in 10-point coated cover stock by McNaughton & Gunn.

The paper used in this publication meets the minimum requirements of American National Standard for Information Sciences—Permanence of Paper for Printed Library Materials, ANSI Z39.48-1992. ∞

**Library of Congress Cataloging-in-Publication Data**

Pfeil, Angela B.
    Going places with youth outreach : smart marketing strategies for your library / by Angela B. Pfeil.
        p.    cm.
    Includes bibliographical references and index.
    ISBN 0-8389-0900-0 (alk. paper)
    1. Children's libraries—United States—Marketing. 2. Library outreach programs—United States. I. Title.
Z718.2.U6P44 2005
021.2'0973—dc22           2005007430

Printed in the United States of America

09   08   07   06   05      5   4   3   2   1

To Laura and Amy.
Hi ladies!

# CONTENTS

# PREFACE

**M**arketing and outreach to children have many similar characteristics. To perform each successfully, your library needs to have a specific plan of implementation that includes who you want to reach, why you should target that group, where the population will be served, what you will market, and when the effort will be implemented. There are many books on library and nonprofit marketing techniques as well as separate titles on outreach to youth. This book supposes that marketing and outreach are intertwined and should be pursued as such. It explores each of the steps required for creating and adhering to a successful marketing and outreach plan for children.

Chapter 1 gives an overview of marketing as it pertains to libraries and, specifically, to youth services. Chapter 2 details the materials that all libraries need to have to successfully implement their marketing programs. Chapter 3 explores existing child-focused library programs that aid in meeting marketing goals and objectives and offers new ideas for outreach as marketing. Chapter 4 discusses using the library website as an important marketing and outreach tool. Chapter 5 delves into the specifics of selling library services to children, parents, and educators. Chapter 6 describes the four distinct parts of any outreach presentation and offers clear guidelines on perfecting each of these phases. Chapter 7 looks at efficient and effective ways of measuring the impact of marketing and outreach efforts. Chapter 8 reviews successful marketing programs from public libraries across the United States. Chapter 9 pulls all the information together using the "Core Competencies of Outreach" as described by author and young adult services consultant Patrick Jones.

This book could not have been written without the unconditional love and devotion from Bob, Alex, Mom, Steve, Stefanie, and Valarie. My sincere thanks go to each of them for understanding the time I needed to write this book and for giving me the encouragement and support for getting it done. Through this book, I share my experiences, thoughts, and ideas about outreach as marketing. Each of my personal values and opinions has been shaped by the various positions I have held, including youth services librarian, community outreach librarian, virtual reference librarian, and cybrary manager. In all of these positions, I served youth outside of the traditional library setting and brought services to where they were. Youth services librarians, reference librarians, library administrators—or any library employee who is involved in planning, implementing, or evaluating services to children—will find this book helpful for understanding what is required of all library staff in order for youth services outreach efforts to be successful.

This book provides an outline for a successful marketing and outreach effort. But even if your library cannot afford or chooses not to support some of the nontraditional ideas for children's programming presented here, it is my hope that you will use what you can to make your library service to youth as successful as possible. Enjoy!

# Introduction

**M**arketing to children often has a negative connotation. Our children are bombarded daily with advertising at school, at home, and on the road. Kids want what is being marketed, and adults quickly determine that the only lasting result of impulse purchases for children is a nation of over-indulged children.

Libraries have always been cornerstones for early literacy programs and have commonly served underserved populations, long before marketing to children became the thing to do. Excessive marketing to children has its consequences, and there is no doubt libraries offer important services for dealing with them. But libraries should also use the existing marketing information, whether it is simple market or demographic research, retail marketing plans, or consumer statistics, to launch full-fledged marketing and outreach efforts of their own. Libraries offer valuable programs, important information, and computer access in-house, but all of these products and services are available only to those existing customers who have transportation to the library.

Marketing library services is more than just publicity and promotion. It's more than just increasing circulation statistics. Marketing is a process that assists libraries in achieving user goals and priorities, satisfying the needs of their users, and attracting new users. In a day and age where budgetary restrictions are reducing staffing and services in many libraries, marketing is an essential tool for building successful relationships with the community. Marketing services to children may be the most powerful but underused part of a library's marketing plan.

Public and school libraries can provide services that benefit the development of children in all communities and from all backgrounds. Through marketing programming, literacy services, and library resources, libraries encourage children to read, to be lifelong library users, and to become responsible and effective users of information. Marketing your library's information services to children will help you maintain and provide essential youth services; moreover, the successful, well-attended, and well-documented programs you offer will justify the requests for increased staff and finances necessary to reach your library goals. Ultimately, you can provide what the youth in your community need and, consequently, increase the productivity and usage of your department and library.

Marketing services to children is not a new concept. For-profit organizations have already recognized the importance of children to the consumer market. Marion Nestle, chair of the Department of Nutrition and Food Studies at New York University, and Margo Wootan estimate that $13 billion a year is spent marketing to American children—by food and drink industries alone. Food advertising makes up about half of all advertising aimed at kids.[1] Children's spending roughly doubled every ten years for the past three decades and tripled in the 1990s. Kids ages four to twelve spent $2.2 billion in 1968 and $4.2 billion in 1984. By 1994 the figure climbed to $17.1 billion, and by 2002 their spending exceeded $40 billion. Kids' direct buying power is expected to exceed $51.8 billion by 2006.[2] In the 1960s children influenced about $5 billion of their parents' purchases. By 1984 that figure increased tenfold, to $50 billion.[3] By 1997 it had tripled to $188 billion. It is clear that children are highly influential in what their parents purchase, and they can exert this same influence with library use.

So, what does this have to do with libraries? Public libraries have always succeeded in attracting new users by using existing data and techniques from similar organizations, that is, "technique sharing." The suggestion that public libraries adopt the best aspects of the typical successful bookstore is an example of technique sharing. Marketing should be no different. If current statistics show that "at six months of age, the same age they are imitating simple sounds like 'ma-ma,' babies are forming mental images of corporate logos and mascots," then the library must adopt a visible and attractive logo and mascot.[4] If, according to recent marketing industry studies, "a person's 'brand loyalty' may begin as early as age two," then libraries have an obligation to be a part of this recognition.[5]

Libraries suffer greatly from budgetary restrictions. Too often, youth services catch the brunt of budget cuts, and the restrictions negatively affect the resources and staffing levels in youth services departments. The library suffers from not being able to provide the services and programming that are so cherished by its community, but a more devastating effect is the lack of education, attention, and nurturing that a library can offer to its young patrons. Marketing services is key to gaining reputability and trust within your community. Those who make decisions regarding your financial status, whether it is a board of directors or taxpayers, need to be shown the importance of libraries. Having a marketing plan in place, and making it your highest priority, will not only increase your internal statistics but also place value on your institution in the eyes of the decision makers. Marketing includes advertising, promotion, publicity, and public relations. The following anecdote helps illustrate this concept:

> If the circus is coming to town and you paint a sign saying, "Circus is coming to Fairgrounds Sunday," that's advertising. If you put the sign on the back of an elephant and walk him through town, that's promotion. If the elephant walks through the mayor's flower bed, and it makes the morning paper, that's publicity. If you can get the mayor to laugh about it, that's public relations. And, if you planned the whole thing, that's marketing!—*Author unknown*

Your library most likely provides children's programming at some point during the year. Story times are a staple of the American public library tradition. According to the National Center for Educational Statistics (NCES), during 2001, nationwide circulation of children's materials was 653.9 million, or 37 percent of total circulation, and attendance at children's programs was 51.8 million. The NCES does not delineate the constitution of "children's programs" among in-house programs, outreach programs, or school visits.[6] The NCES does, however, classify Family Literacy and programs aimed at parents as Adult Literacy Programs, according to their report "Programs for

Adults in Public Library Outlets."[7] Although most youth services departments provide the Family Literacy programming, the purpose of those presentations is to hook the parent, not the child. This may be one of the reasons that NCES classifies them as Adult Literacy Programs.

*Going Places with Youth Outreach* seeks to help libraries create, plan, and evaluate current and future youth marketing and outreach efforts. The purpose is to educate librarians on the marketing process as well as to empower them to try new ideas for reaching out to children.

## NOTES

1. Marion Nestle and Margo Wootan, "Spending on Marketing to Kids Up $5 Billion in Last Decade," *Food Institute Report*, April 15, 2002.
2. James McNeal, *The Kids Market: Myths and Realities* (Ithaca, NY: Paramount Market, 1999).
3. James McNeal, "Tapping the Three Kids' Markets," *American Demographics*, April 1998.
4. James McNeal and Chyon-Hwa Yeh, "Born to Shop," *American Demographics*, June 1993.
5. "Brand Aware," *Children's Business*, June 2000.
6. National Center for Educational Statistics, Library Statistics Program, "Public Libraries in the United States: Fiscal Year 2001." Available from http://nces.ed.gov/pubs2003/2003399.pdf.
7. National Center for Educational Statistics. "Programs for Adults in Public Library Outlets." Available from http://nces.ed.gov/pubs2003/2003010.pdf.

*Chapter One*

# What Is Marketing?

**M**arketing seems to be the new buzzword in libraries. A quick glance at the new literature shows numerous publications specifically about promoting your library. What exactly is marketing? Merriam-Webster's Online Dictionary defines *marketing* as follows:

> 1 a: the act or process of selling or purchasing in a market b: the process or technique of promoting, selling, and distributing a product or service.[1]

Traditionally, marketing uses the "marketing mix," or the "Four *P*s": product, pricing, place, and promotion. Some marketing professionals enhance the mix to "Five *P*s," to include people, or "Seven *P*s," to include physical evidence and process. This chapter explores the Five *P*s. Each of these *P*s is an element in the mix. To help explain a marketing mix, think of a cake mix. Every cake includes eggs, milk, flour, and sugar. You can change the taste and texture of the cake by increasing or decreasing one or more of these ingredients. If you want a sweeter cake, add more sugar. If you want a drier cake, add more flour. This concept of changing the final product by emphasizing elements of the mix—in this case, product, pricing, place, promotion, and people—applies to marketing.

## In the Mix

Let's take a closer look at the elements of the marketing mix.

## Product

Products are typically introduced into the market after a period of development. Throughout the growth stage, the product gains more and more customers. The market stabilizes through the maturity stage. After a period of time in the maturity stage, the product is met with competition and may continue to develop, but, eventually, many products begin to decline and eventually withdraw. It is important to know that most products fail in the introduction stage. Your product may not have been successful, but you have not yet invested much time and money, and a positive change can still be made. Know that yours is not the only product or service to be reevaluated in this phase.

For libraries, products may include materials (books, videos, recordings, etc.) and services (story times, bibliographic instruction, demonstrations, exhibits, etc.). The range of products offered is, or should be, directly related to the organization's mission and goals. As with any product, library products must be fully developed before they are introduced to the consumer. Librarians have been providing story times, class visits, and special programs for the children in their communities for a very long time. It is safe to say that these service concepts have been fully developed.

## Price

The price for library services cannot be defined using the traditional pricing strategies. For-profit companies set a price based on what the product is worth and what people are willing to pay. Library services are most often free, so libraries can either be said to have set pricing or to be priceless. Even when there is no charge for services, price is not something to leave out when promoting them. Saying the word *free* to a group of consumers will most often turn heads and get their attention, especially children. Price for library services must include the cost of staff to support the project as well as any other materials (including books, computers, puppets, or supplies) needed for the effort. Many youth outreach initiatives begin as pilot projects funded through outside agencies. Unfortunately, many of these projects end when the funding period is over, or they change completely to meet the needs dictated by a new funding agency. Library administration needs to consider the cost of maintaining a successful program before engaging in externally funded programs.

## Place

Place is simply defined for libraries. You will either offer services in the main library or a branch, or you will reach out to the public through partnerships with community agencies. All library outreach services should be direct to consumer, meaning that you go to where the consumers are. Library marketing efforts and services must go beyond the walls of the library to be effective. One intermediary a library may use is its own website. Online outreach will be discussed in chapter 4.

## Promotion

Promotion is intended to facilitate the communication between the information agency and its target audience. Effective communication is only achieved when a message is received, understood, accepted, and correctly acted upon. The sender of a message is identified as the organization trying to disseminate information about a product. The message must be clear, unambiguous, and acceptable to the receiver. In selecting a medium, organizations can choose from personal selling, sales promotion, public relations, trade fairs, advertising, or sponsorship. Once the message is sent, the receiver must be able to decode it accurately. The intended receiver is the most important role in this communications process. It is imperative that the information is directed to receivers in a way they can comprehend. Feedback should evaluate not only whether a message is being acted upon but also why or why not. When promoting library services to children, this communications process is most important. The message must be on a level that they can understand, and it also must appeal to some basic need or desire they have. When promoting library services, you must use lay terms rather than librarianese, especially when promoting to children.

## People

People are the core of libraries. This *P* is sometimes added to the marketing mix to recognize the importance of the human element in all aspects of marketing. For libraries, people are the key to marketing. Larger libraries often have a community relations, public relations, or marketing person or department on staff. Marketing professionals have a wealth of knowledge, and often an address book filled with community contacts, and should be respected for this. These professionals are important, yet they should be involved in but not responsible for all library marketing services. Too often, there is a community relations person speaking to groups or being interviewed on television about the library. Although these marketing professionals' support is imperative, the library is better served by sending a face that customers will recognize. This factor is especially important when promoting services to children. Children love to recognize people when they go places, especially somewhere new. This identification gives them a sense of belonging and attachment to the visited place. If you are in youth services, you know how excited a child is to see you again after a class visit. Thus does outreach become marketing, with the library gaining happy young customers (to grow into happy older customers).

Marketing is outreach in that you are reaching out to a target audience with the goal of informing them of your products. Librarians who do outreach are marketing the library. Whether yours is a small or a large library, for outreach efforts to be successful, you need to define the goals and clarify the objectives of the program.

## Marketing Goals and Objectives

Marketing library services to children involves the same strategies as marketing to adults. Steps for marketing include identifying objectives; analyzing the market to be reached, including the market's strengths, weaknesses, threats, and opportunities; and marketing to the community by recognizing and targeting the market mix as well as its segmentation. Any marketing plan should have no more than three specific goals. Goals can be defined as the destination, and objectives are the way to get there. For each goal, delineate specific objectives.

### Identifying Objectives

Identifying objectives is the first and most important step when beginning a new marketing program. Objectives should be defined for the budget, staff, and programs. Rational, obtainable objectives serve as guidelines for programming as well as a measuring tool for tracking progress. Objectives should be as detailed as possible.

## BUDGETARY OBJECTIVES

Any outreach program will have a budget, no matter how large or small. It is necessary to define and delineate the budget externally, through the sponsoring agency, as well as internally, through the library district. With budget restrictions and reduced income to library districts, staff may need to seek out other forms of funding, such as grants. Grants offer an extra benefit: throughout the grant-writing process, many of the objectives need to be specifically stated, thus giving the team a head start in defining these goals. When stating budgetary objectives, be specific. Think about everything in your program that will cost money. Materials should be clearly defined and prices researched. For example, if you plan to purchase puppets, look at vendor catalogs so you can create a budget that reflects current prices. Budgetary objectives will be explored again in chapter 5.

## STAFF OBJECTIVES

New programs often cause a strain on existing staff in libraries. There are times when new positions are created through external funding sources, but more often staff are redistributed to create positions for a new department, or the additional duties are spread among existing staff. If the intent is to use branch library children's staff to implement a whole library program, for example, it is important to remember that not all staff will view the increased duties as a bonus. When preparing staffing objectives, whether to create a new team of outreach specialists or to have existing staff reach out as part of their jobs, be specific about what is expected and explain the change in duties.

Not only is the number of staff important but their abilities as well. Should the decision be to present assemblies to large groups of children, staff with fear of public speaking or who are extremely uncomfortable in front of big crowds should not be involved in those aspects of promotion. Job descriptions of staffers on this team should be specifically written to address the goals and objectives of the program.

Marketing professionals have perfected the art of public presentation and persuasion. Outreach staff should have some of the qualities of successful marketers, which include a positive attitude, personal integrity, a belief in and passion for the product, organization and preparation skills, and an appreciation for the audience. These qualities are often placed second to knowledge of children's literature when libraries hire youth services staff, but they need to be priority qualities when defining the outreach team. Staffing objectives will be explored again in chapter 5.

### PROGRAM OBJECTIVES

Program objectives should state who will be targeted, where the programs will be presented, and the total number of programs planned. These are specific, quantifiable objectives, but your program should also have emotional, or qualitative, objectives. Clarify what you expect the audience to learn from your program, whether it is simply the name of the library or how to use the library's services. Programming for name recognition is quite different from programming for information literacy. Know what your specific program objectives are and how to achieve that goal. Program objectives are often changed and become more specific as outreach continues.

## Market Analysis

A market analysis, whether formal or informal, is necessary to set specific staffing and program objectives. Your library may simply not have the money to support a formal market analysis, but the outreach librarian is still responsible for understanding the community. Informal market analyses can be done on the drive to work, through a walk around the neighborhood, or by looking through the local community agency directory. Whether this analysis is done over an extended period of time with a large budget or on your lunch break with no budget, you will still have identified local, nearby community agencies, schools, and other businesses that are all potential partners.

Libraries need to know what programs are already available (or unavailable), who is providing them, and how they can help with existing programs or fill the need for new ones. Library districts often have a defined community that they serve, whether based on tax revenue or simple map grids. Use this existing information to primarily define your market in terms of the following agencies and programs.

## Community Agencies

Boys and Girls Clubs, Head Start Programs, local YMCAs and YWCAs, and city and county recreational facilities are all based on the notion of helping children become effective citizens. Although each agency offers different types of programs, they all share waning budgets and face the risks of overcrowded programs. Invest in these agencies by including programs for them in your marketing plan.

## Elementary and Middle Schools

Teachers and school administrators are always on the lookout for free, educational, and time-saving materials and presentations to use in their classrooms. Identify the schools in your area that seem to be most receptive or show the most need, and approach them with ideas of how you can help them. Before targeting services to elementary and middle schools, obtain personal contact information for teachers and administrators to ensure your programs are applicable.

## Other Existing Businesses

Each community has its own notable community partners, many of whom are for-profit agencies that are already deeply entrenched in their own marketing plans. As noted earlier, companies spend a lot of money to determine who is not using their services as well as how to improve services to existing customers, so they are often interested in working with nonprofit agencies to bring additional value to their customers. Partnering with these agencies comes at a cost—and that is the cost of adding their name next to yours on all materials produced for the particular program! This is a small price to pay to be able to reach new audiences.

Once you have created an inventory list of potential community partners, you must research each company's mission and vision statements. Be sure the agencies you work with are reputable and that they understand your mission and vision statements also. Know what specific programs are already being offered. Realize the potential for enhancing current community programs as well as filling an evident void in necessary programming. After you have done your research, you will need to network with those potential partners.

## Community Networking

In sales, calling a potential customer without warning is known as a cold call. The last thing you want to do is to approach your potential partnership agencies by cold-calling them. Instead, spend time speaking with leaders in other educational institutions, whether at conferences, staff training, awards ceremonies, board meetings, or at your local coffee shop. These informal meetings will prove to be the biggest asset in your advocacy approach. Although networking is most likely done between adults, it is possible, and quite wise, to network with children. Networking with children can occur any time and any place, just like networking with adults. When you visit a school and are greeted in the hallway by a student, take a moment to get his or her name, and give the student yours. When you are at places geared toward children, such as a park or playground, be visible but not intrusive. Talk with the lingering parents also. Remember that every opportunity for community networking should be treated as an interview. Use common and proven interview techniques.

> *Dress for success.* Dressing for success doesn't mean you need to wear a suit but rather just look nice. Wear some sort of library identifying information but *not* your staff badge. If your library has pins or shirts decorated with the library logo, choose to wear such items when networking.
>
> *Smile.* Yes, smile. People are sent out into the community to represent the agency, and your agency is judged by those representatives. If your outreach specialist is in a meeting consumed in a book or scowling at the presenter, your whole agency will be perceived this way. Smile, whether you like what they are saying or not.
>
> *Ask questions.* Show interest in what is being said and ask pertinent questions.
>
> *Solicit contact information.* Trade business cards when the meeting is over.

### Community Agencies and Educational Institutions

Networking with community agencies and educational institutions may require a bit of sleuthing. Access websites or visit local headquarters for more information about upcoming events, and then attend them. Read the newspapers, attend city council meetings, and make yourself known to these other influential people in your community. Don't attend empty-handed. Be prepared to hand out a business card, and if you have novelty items with your library's identifying information on them, people can take them back to their offices as a reminder of the library and its services (see chapter 2 for more discussion of novelty marketing materials). Finally, follow up your informal meeting with an e-mail thanking them for their time and offering your assistance. And remember to treat every contact as an agency interview.

Most importantly, when networking in your community, send the right person. If your library is fortunate enough to have a personable, knowledgeable, and professional community outreach librarian on staff, make community-networking time part of his or her duties. If not, be sure that all staff members representing the library are trained in the same way on library policies and that all understand and can relay these institutional goals quickly and effectively.

## Politicians and Religious Leaders

Be sure to keep up with your local community leaders and events they are sponsoring. Many communities hold parades, host farmers' markets, and offer family programming with the support of other local governmental agencies. Be a part of those events.

Many religious organizations offer their followers services that may include day care (for example, a mom's night/day out). Although parishioners are happy to support these events by donating their time, what a relief it would be for them, and a treat for the children, to have a special story-time visitor.

■ ■ ■ ■ ■

In any networking situation, you are acting as your agency's representative. If you are unclear about your own library's mission and vision, be sure to completely understand them before trying to explain them to others. The library's marketing plan should encompass and expand upon the mission and vision statements.

## Marketing Plan

Your marketing and outreach plan is more than a mission statement. Each of the elements in the marketing mix, as well as your goals and objectives, will result in your marketing plan. Every plan should be written down and distributed to—and understood by—all staff members. It should include all related district priorities determined through internal and external strategic-planning processes. It ought to include timelines and dates for meeting those goals and objectives. Marketing plans use simple storytelling techniques. Find the answers to the basic questions of who, what, where, why, when, and how, and you will have the library marketing story.

## Who are we trying to reach?

Libraries serve all people. When developing an outreach effort, your "who" should be specific. If your goal is to reach elementary school children, it should say so. If there are specific populations within that group, be sure to note that.

## What are we trying to do?

Will you be promoting the library? What will you promote? Story times, electronic resources, fiction titles, computer use, the library website? Be very specific in what you are trying to do. Know your product, and then articulate it.

## Where are we going to do it?

Will you go to schools or other community agencies? Are you already going there? Use the inventory list you created when you were evaluating the existing market for possible partnerships. If possible, when contacting the agencies, try to rank their enthusiasm and willingness to work with you. The most enthusiastic groups should be your first contacts.

## Why are we doing it?

Identify the need that has been determined.

## When is it done?

Will it be in the evenings, mornings, after school? Be sure to consider the staffing for the project. Will it be shared staffing (a team comprised of members from various library locations) or private staffing (a team dedicated to only the efforts of this program)? When are the team members available? What are their schedules?

## How will we afford it?

Where is the funding coming from? What is funded? Are staff members included? How will the library afford staff through either reallocation or creating new positions?

■ ■ ■ ■ ■

Yes, this is a book about marketing to children, and you are well on your way to exploring new ideas for your library. Keep in mind that although you have to sell your service ideas to adults, the service will benefit the children. By identifying your objectives, conducting a market analysis, using powerful community networking, and creating a marketing plan, you will have already presold your service. Now, it's time to deliver.

NOTE

1. Merriam-Webster's Online Dictionary. Available from http://www.m-w.com.

*Chapter Two*

# Marketing Materials

**A**ll traditional library promotional literature should be considered marketing materials. Every library has printed materials available to the public. Some libraries have too much information displayed, and others do not have enough. Quantity of materials matters, and so does creating a consistent visual image on each item. Having a strong, consistent visual image will enhance your visibility and your viability, especially to children.

## Library Logo

In most large corporations, the logo is at the center of their marketing plans. It is usually designed by graphic designers, with input and approval from the management team. Libraries are no different. Library logos should play an instrumental role in identifying library-related informational materials. The logo should, in a small graphic, depict the value, worth, and mission statement of the library as well as the library name or initials. Choosing a color scheme for the logo is as important as the logo itself. The identified color scheme is one that will have to match the personality of the library and catch the reader's attention. In general marketing practices, the base logo is improved upon to reach certain audiences or to show special sales or events. The library logo should be versatile enough to be attractive to children as well as adults.

The Las Vegas–Clark County Library District (figure 2.1) in Nevada has a logo that is easily recognized by both children and adults. The graphic of a dark brown, large, book-shaped building with light emerging from the open door placed directly next to the name of the library district in a clear font can be easily modified for various purposes. It can be placed on numerous background colors and is simple enough to accommodate other information or graphics. This simple yet powerful logo portrays an open-door policy as well as the symbolic enlightenment of any user through the bright light emerging from the open door. With

**Figure 2.1**

its book-shaped building, this logo encompasses the traditional idea of what a library is, a building with books.

The Hennepin County Library (Minnesota) logo is quite different (see figure 2.2). Rather than focusing on the library as a building, it uses a person-centered approach, with a joyous human figure dancing with—or perhaps jumping up to grab hold of—a book. This action-packed, empowering image conveys a feeling of excitement about the library. This image, placed next to the name of the library district, which is written in a clear and concise font, is easily recognized and accepted. Both the text and the image's outline are white on a red background.

**Figure 2.2**

In both cases, the logo incorporates the name of the library district and, most importantly, uses an increased font size for the word *Library*.

Once your library has identified its logo, it should be used on everything visibly available to the public. This would include library cards, summer reading program T-shirts, the website, and all library correspondence. The logo can be the library's greatest asset, especially when marketing to children. Because they are visual learners—

in part because of their developmentally low reading ability—children identify images with content. McDonald's, for example, is recognized by children worldwide because of its golden arches.

## Library Information Materials

All libraries produce promotional brochures, flyers, bookmarks, and newsletters. Although most often these materials are left in the branches to be picked up by existing users, it is imperative that the following materials be available in large quantities as they can be used in your outreach marketing efforts.

### Map of Locations

A map illustrating the library's main and branch locations shows the customer what libraries are available to them and where they are located. It should be as clear as possible, with major cross streets listed by each identified location as well as an easy-to-read key to locations. The map should also include contact information and library hours for each of the branches. This promotional item has many uses besides directing customers to other locations. For example, see figure 2.3, Las Vegas–Clark County Library District's pamphlet "A Parent's Guide to Using the Library."

This pamphlet is printed on glossy paper in full color. The graphic uses bright colors, such as orange for the lizard, yellow for the background, olive green for the text at the bottom, and purple as the background for the library card.

The Las Vegas–Clark County Library District creates two of these pamphlets, one for adults and one for adults with children. The adult pamphlet is intended to be read by parents, yet it is visually appealing to children, and they may pick it up simply for its look. Some of the pamphlet content differs, but it is clear that the district recognizes the importance of locating libraries, as shown by the map on the last page in each of these brochures.

### How to Get a Library Card,
### with Library Card Application

A brochure about getting a library card contains especially important information. It should include simple instructions about acquiring

Figure 2.3

and using a library card. Start with a general statement about what privileges come with a library card, such as loan periods, borrowing limits, and materials available. Ensure that an application is attached. When the brochures are used in outreach efforts, they can be easily returned to the closest library. Rather than printing two separate pieces, you may choose to print this and the locations map in one pamphlet.

## Library Card

The library card, the staple of the American library tradition, can be a marketing tool if it is strategically located. Many public libraries have begun issuing key-chain cards, ones that are hole punched and small enough to carry on a key ring. Whenever the customers' keys are out of their pockets or purses, anyone around may notice and ask what these colorful key-chain cards are for. Typically, these key-ring cards are formatted like the store-brand cards used in the same way, with the identifying logo on one side and the account or library card number on the other. Even though children may not have car keys, with the rise in working parents, most school-age children do carry a house key or bike-lock key with them on a daily basis. They would appreciate having this small library card so their key rings can look just like their parent's. Parents appreciate carrying their children's cards on their key rings so they don't have to try and find them before going to the library.

### SAMPLE LIBRARY CARDS

*Las Vegas–Clark County Library District*

The Las Vegas–Clark County Library District adult library card is black, with the library logo and website featured on the front of the card (see figure 2.4). The book and building part of the logo is in a deep brown, and both the light emerging from the building as well as the text of the library name and website are featured in a muted yet prominent yellow tone.

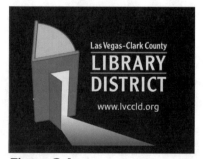

**Figure 2.4**

The children's card is purple and does not feature the standard library logo. Rather, it features the library mascot, "Neon," holding a book (see figure 2.5). Neon is mostly orange, with yellow on his belly, and wears green sunglasses. The book he holds is brown in color. Staying with the vibrant color scheme, yet still true to

**Figure 2.5**

its adult counterpart, the library name is in a prominent yellow tone, although here it is almost fluorescent. The library website is also listed and uses a muted fluorescent green as its color. Both library cards are offered as key-chain cards as well.

### Henderson District Public Libraries

Using a simple color scheme of purples and oranges, the Henderson District Public Libraries (Nevada) distinctly features their logo next to a graphic image of a seeming sunrise behind the mountains (see figure 2.6). This card is simple and clear,

**Figure 2.6**

and the name of the library district is printed at the bottom of the card in a clear font. The library web address is in bold type on the back of the card.

### Hennepin County Library

The Hennepin County Library standard card features a calming color scheme of mauve, lilac, aqua, and beige, with a subtle image of a book at the lower left corner, the library logo in the upper left corner, and the word *Welcome* restated in seven languages other than English (see figure 2.7). At the center of the card is a recognizable satellite image of the world, with the library website beginning on that image and following to the right.

**Figure 2.7**

*King County Library System*

The King County Library System (Washington) offers its customers a choice of five different library cards, and two are featured here. Each of the cards is available as a traditional library card and as a key-chain card. All of the library cards feature the library logo at the center of the card, with a motto, "Turn to us. The choices will surprise you," running across the top and crossing both the image and the color background.

One popular card features an image of a hand reaching out (see figure 2.8). The image portrays activity rather than passivity. This library card is primarily black but very eye-catching.

**Figure 2.8**

Another popular King County Library System card, featuring young people wearing 3-D glasses, seems to be made specifically for youth (see figure 2.9). Wearing 3-D glasses is always fun for young-sters, but the underlying meaning of bringing the library to life is most important. The major color of this library card is blue.

**Figure 2.9**

## Newsletters

Library newsletters are easy to produce. Typically, this type of library publication is used to retain current customers rather than attract new ones. Some larger library districts produce two separate newsletters, one for adults and one for children. Unfortunately, it is usually the adult newsletter that is mass mailed. Why not send the children their own newsletter to look through? It will remind them of the library and give them something to use to remind their parents. Kids love getting mail, and this is one piece that will educate them. If your library is unable to specifically mail a newsletter to children either because of limited report features in your software or because you have a library policy statement about not targeting children, create a newsletter for adults who work with children, specifically teachers, day-care providers, or pediatricians.

The Multnomah County Library (Oregon) School Corps issues its "School Corps Quarterly" newsletter to targeted service populations (see figure 2.10). This newsletter calls attention to children's programs, curriculum-relevant resources, and services offered by the School Corps staff. Its simple layout, with short text pieces and appropriate graphics, is both aesthetic and educational.

Newsletters can effectively disseminate timely information about programs, resources, and services. Clean lines and a large font are essential. Too much information in too little space will certainly be visually overwhelming. When producing for kids, use graphics to supplement the content. For example, if you are promoting science programs, use pictures of such science-related items as beakers and microscopes.

## Bookmarks

Libraries love producing bookmarks—on popular topics, new books, old books, electronic resources, and any other applicable subject or genre. Although bookmarks from libraries is a great concept, any item in overabundance will not be picked up or used as it should— simple supply and demand. If a child sees one bookmark waiting on a "Take Me" table, he or she is apt to grab it up and hold it with pride. When children see four different bookmarks in large stacks, they look through for more and usually make a mess of the display area. If you

**Multnomah County Library**

# School Corps Quarterly

An occasional publication of the Multnomah County Library School Corps — an outreach program connecting students, teachers and media staff with public library resources

*School Corps Quarterly, December 2004*                                    *Volume 6, Issue 2*

## School Corps Presentations for Staff
*by Sara Ryan*

Does your school have an in-service day or a department meeting coming up? School Corps can present any of our technology trainings to teachers as well as to students. Find a list of School Corps trainings at www.multcolib.org/schoolcorps/menu.html. With a library catalog training, teachers can learn how to quickly find:

- Bestsellers
- Books in series
- Movies
- Music
- Materials in languages other than English

Teachers can also learn how to request multiple copies of library materials, renew items online, and place holds on material that's on order.

A training about Multnomah County Library's Web sites can help teachers to:

- Find out about upcoming library events and programs, and sign up for classes online
- Learn which of our subscription databases are most useful and relevant
- Save time with "self-service" booklists
- Check the hours at your neighborhood library
- And much more!

School Corps can also booktalk hot new titles, current award winners, or books that have been nominated for awards.

If you're interested in having a School Corps librarian come to an in-service day, staff or department meeting, please contact Jackie Partch at 503.988.6004 or jacquelp@multcolib.org.

## Rolie Polie Olie and Dinosaur Bob Coming to the Library!
*by Katie O'Dell*

Welcome to the weird, wild world of William Joyce! You and your students will have the chance to see original art by the talented creator on display at Multnomah County Library. *The World of William Joyce* will be on display in the Central Library Collins Gallery from February 17 until April 12, 2005.

Students of all ages will marvel at the multimedia and eye-popping work, and those interested in both illustration and computer animation will be especially engaged! A self-guided tour, including books to share with your students, will be available to groups. All groups who take the self-guided tour will receive complimentary William Joyce buttons for their students! Call 503.988.5340 to reserve your tour time.

### Everybody Reads 2005

*The House on Mango Street* by Sandra Cisneros is the 2005 Everybody Reads selection. A series of vignettes about a young woman growing up in a Hispanic neighborhood in Chicago, the book is listed on many recommended reading lists for high school students.

The goal of the annual Everybody Reads project is to encourage the entire community to read a single work of literature and discuss it with others. Numerous events exploring Sandra Cisneros and her work will take place during late January and February 2005, including an open-mike program where teens can share their poetry, prose or artwork inspired by *The House on Mango Street.*

Find out more about Everybody Reads and related events at www.multcolib.org/reads/.

*For more information, call Jackie Partch at 503.988.6004 or e-mail jacquelp@multcolib.org*

**Figure 2.10**

choose to display multiple bookmarks, it is best to keep the piles at roughly the same height (one-inch stacks work best). If possible, display bookmarks throughout the children's area, including specific sections of the book stacks where they may be more helpful. (For example, if you have bookmarks about science experiments, place them near the books on science experiments.) Bookmarks should be simply made, with relatively lightweight paper, and should not necessarily need approval from library administration or the graphic arts department to be produced. These are simple items that can be easily formatted, printed, and cut in a local branch using existing desktop-publishing software that many staff have access to. Regardless of who creates and prints these, the library logo should be present on each bookmark.

## Business Cards

With shrinking budgets, one way libraries are cutting costs is by reducing the number of business cards produced for staff members. Business cards serve more purposes than creating a feeling of self-worth among staff. When staff business cards are emblazoned with the library logo, library website, and specific contact information for the library, they are one of the library's biggest promotional tools. Not only are the sizes of business cards suitable for easy transport but the cards are also constant reminders of the library as they are usually kept in a wallet or billfold that is accessed daily. Make your business cards look like a library card. Rather than printing the contact information on the front, put it on the back. Your library card art has probably already been created and can now be used for more than one purpose.

Chapter 3 discusses using these existing items as marketing tools and in successful outreach programs to children.

## Novelty Library Materials

When libraries put on a special event or a special session of programming, often a novelty item is budgeted for and purchased to either give away or sell to the attendees. There are companies who work primarily with libraries in developing new and innovative items to distribute. The JanWay Corporation has been at the heart of custom library promotions since the company's inception in 1981. Its website (http://www.janway.com) offers easy navigability as well as unique ideas for library promotions. K-READ Custom Promotions offers a special "Reading Store" with library- and literacy-related items. Its website (http://www.k-read.net) is searchable by type of promotion as well as by keyword. Although capturing library users' attention is important, the marketing plan may call for attracting new users. Using novelty, or nontraditional, items may be most effective.

## Pencils and Pens

Pencils are relatively inexpensive, even when they are special ordered and designed to your specifications. One drawback to using pencils as a novelty item is the small amount of display space on the pencil for information. When using pencils, it is best to display the library or outreach program name and a web address. Pencils are easy to distribute and are necessary for most students in elementary school. If your library purchases pens to distribute and plans on giving them out at elementary schools, be sure that the color of the ink is the same as the mandatory ink color most schools require. Although the colorful and popular gel pens may seem to be more attractive to students, these will not be used for schoolwork and therefore may not be used on a daily basis. Distributing pencils and pens to children doubly benefits the library because they serve an educational need and the library marketing plan.

## Stickers

Kids love stickers. Some children collect stickers, while others simply like to display them on notebooks, artwork, and in their homes. Distributing visually appealing library stickers will be a huge success with children. These stickers should be no larger than 3 x 3 inches, and they should include the library logo along with any other special library information, such as the kids' website or the name of the special outreach program. Some libraries create bookplate stickers for distribution. Kids can then apply these to the books in their personal libraries. Although this is a worthwhile idea, how often are kids going to look at the stickers on the inside covers of books they are not reading anymore? However you choose to format these stickers, it is important to remember your library's mission statement and purpose for printing the stickers. These stickers can be distributed as prizes for ongoing reading programs and can also be used to distribute during outreach. Although these are not serving any educational need of students, they will foster the brand recognition that the library is looking to attain.

## Book Covers

Many schools require or encourage their students to cover their text-books. Parents scramble around to find the perfect paper, and teachers usually only have a limited supply of book covers. Creating book covers with library information, including useful library links, books, or e-resources related to the subject, and distributing these free to schools will meet the needs of the students and take a burden off of the parents. When making book covers, be creative. You can create one layout that includes all the subjects, or you may choose to do different layouts for each of the subjects. All book covers may be printed on the same paper, or, if the covers are already separated by subject, each subject may be printed in a different color. Book covers remind students of the library daily.

## Posters

Many libraries deem posters as too expensive to create and prefer to use the free posters librarians receive at local and national conferences or to purchase the standard READ posters from the American Library Association. These posters serve an important, dual purpose by showing celebrities reading and by promoting all sorts of books. Posters created by your library will serve the important purpose of promoting your library specifically. Be sure to include such information as the library logo, library website, address, and phone number. It's best to feature actual images of kids using the library or of staff performing a program. As with any large sign, these posters should be colorful, inviting, and intriguing. Teachers will gladly accept and display the library's promotional poster. Kids will see the poster each day, and when it comes time to prepare reports or projects, they will know they have a library they can go to.

## Folders

Every student needs a folder at some point in the school year. Try producing a plain, colored folder with the library district logo in a visible but not overwhelming spot on the cover. Include suggested resource lists for various subjects on the inside, and this folder will meet the needs of both students and the library marketing plan. When creating content for the inside of the folder, remember to include the library web address and specific directions on how to access the featured resources. If possible, create folders that have a perforated insert for business cards, and encourage students to keep their library cards in that spot.

## Key Chains

When you offer key-chain library cards, why not offer students a key chain for the cards? They will leave your library with a set of keys more rewarding and empowering than any set of car keys—you are giving them the keys to unlock the door to information.

## Other Novelty Items

Anything that kids collect, no matter how small, can be created with the library logo on it. Consider yo-yos, pencil sharpeners, rulers, pencil cases, notebooks, book bags, temporary tattoos, magnets, and other items for your library promotions.

Marketing materials can be large or small, and they can meet a need or simply fulfill a desire. Whatever your library chooses to produce, be sure that it is not only a quality product but also one that meets the objectives of the marketing plan. Remember to include the library logo, name, and website on all materials.

*Chapter Three*

# Outreach
# Is Marketing

**M**arketing children's library services is not just sitting at a booth at an exhibit or event telling people who happen to stop by about your services. Although creating awareness through large community events is a grand idea, it should not be the focus of your efforts. Being an exhibitor allows you to fully distribute information to a very unspecific population. If your marketing plan is to simply hand out library materials, then exhibit booths are a perfect place. However, if your plan specifically uses the words *educate, learner, successful,* or *outreach,* then your staff will need to be more active than simply sitting at a booth. Anyone can sit at a booth, smile, and give out freebies, but only specially trained and enthusiastic staff can appropriately market your products and services. With the restraints on library staff and budgets, it only makes sense to use programs already in place to begin to market to children.

The examples that follow include both traditional children's programs and new, nontraditional programs. In each, the first point of contact, and the person you need to convince most about the need for your service, is typically an adult—just as Disney and Nickelodeon depend on the parent to purchase the television. Once the sale has been made, however, the focus is all about the kids. Let's take a look first at what librarians are already doing to market library services to children, and then let's look at some new ideas.

## Traditional Children's Library Programs

### In-House Programs

Youth services staff have always provided educational, literacy-based programs in the library. Although parents are necessary for transportation to and from story times, and they often sit with the children during story times, these programs are created for the child. Likewise, library marketing efforts should be child centered. You probably inform parents about these events through a library publication, direct mailing, public-service announcements, or simply through in-house signage at your library. When the announcements are created, they are commonly in print format, with few or no pictures used. Wouldn't it be wonderful if you had a sign posted for the program that the child approached and identified with? Where are your announcements posted, and at what height? Are they at adult eye level, or low to the ground? Are they in a place where only adults visit, or can they be accessed by children? With all the current information we have about the influence of a child on an adult's purchase, flyers, announcements, and posters that provide information about your programs should be where the child will see them.

The programs provided in the library can be age specific and age appropriate, theme based and need based. For example, for a preschool program with an apple theme, youth services staff spend hours carefully planning each presentation by reading all the picture books about apples, finding apple finger plays, and deciding on a developmentally appropriate apple-themed craft while at the same time staffing a reference desk. When it is time for the program, another staff member covers the desk so the presenter can perform without distraction. Have you ever asked the desk staff how many children they served during your story time? Time spent preparing in-house programming is often justified because these programs increase many different statistics for the library, such as number of people visiting the library, number of books circulated, and number of children attending the program. Remember, though, if you are only promoting literacy, reading, and information services in your branches, you are missing out on a large audience.

## Summer Reading Program

One priority that seems to remain the same each year in public libraries is the juvenile summer reading program. Library staff spend many hours working on the "perfect" theme or coming up with the "ultimate" program. Then staff move on to creating programs, distributing promotional and informational materials, and gathering prizes that meet the needs of the program. Typically, summer reading programs last as long as a traditional story-time session, but there is much more emphasis placed and money spent on this event. Library literature is now investigating the feasibility of these programs, and some have called for the summer reading programs to stop altogether. Think about all of the staff time spent planning for this event. Now think about how many more children actually participate in this program compared to other sessions of the same length. Is it worth it? If your youth services staff are like so many other districts' staff, they probably spend many hours of outreach time (out-of-branch, off-desk time) performing, reciting, and promoting the summer reading program in local schools. If your summer reading program's in-house participation is larger than most other times of the year, think about why. If the rest of your programs were promoted as heavily, they too would yield a higher attendance.

## Class Presentations

Teachers often want to bring their students to the library or have the librarian visit the classroom, and these are services the public librarian should offer. Too often, however, it is the teacher or school that initiates this request. Do the teachers in your local school district know that you offer class visits and will go to their classrooms and promote the library? If the library is not proactive in marketing this service, it may not happen.

How many school-age children actually visit the library before 3 p.m., or during the school day? Compare this to how many schoolchildren you would reach if you went to where they are. Even in places with year-round schools, there are times during the day when there are no children at the library.

While promoting your class-visit service, it is most helpful if you include information on how it fits into the school curriculum. Curriculum handbooks are readily available by calling the school district that you serve or by visiting the district's website. When you ask teachers to take time out of their busy days for a visit from you, it is important that they get something out of the visit, too. Teachers will benefit from your helping them meet a curricular need, provide information to students on a current project, or simply promote literacy.

Getting teachers excited about the library is the key to getting into their classrooms. Knowing what excites them, *free* educational programming, will get you in. It is never a good idea to approach class visits in a selfish way, through saying things like "Kids *need* to know about the library" or "One of our goals this year is to visit every first-grade class." Although some teachers will respond to these statements, some may feel obligated to have you visit, and do you really want to spend time at a school that doesn't really want you there but invited you simply to help you meet your goal? Finally, even though your entire focus ought to be on the children during the presentation, don't forget to thank the teacher for having you.

## Day-Care Centers

With day-care attendance rising, in both home-based and corporate facilities, young children are simply unable to come to the library. Librarians and professional organizations have recognized this and have started many preschool literacy initiatives. Like arranging visits in elementary school classrooms, day-care-center visits are almost always initiated by the teacher or aide who is familiar with the library's services. The same day-care centers are visited over and over again. Think about what centers, and thus children, are being missed in your community. Market your services to them. Rarely is marketing a plan of retention but rather one of gaining attention. Once you are there, you are engaging the attention of preschoolers, not of teachers. You are promoting literacy to children.

## Community Centers

Often the neglected recipients of outreach services, community centers such as Boys and Girls Clubs, recreational centers, and local parks see a high number of visits from school-age children without their parents. One premise of these centers is to provide a safe place for children to go. Very often, these centers seek out special guests and speakers to expose the attending children to a wide range of activities and to lessen the daily workload of the staff. Because they, like public libraries, are often unsure about future funding, they are always looking for free services. Too often, the library is never considered to be a part of their yearly activities for the simple reason that the administrators of these programs are not aware of services the library offers outside of the physical library building. Like class visits at schools, public libraries may benefit from knowing the goals of the organization and figuring out where the library fits in. Once this is decided, a letter or flyer can be sent, a phone call made, or a library staff member can just drop in to the center. Although you have to hook the adults involved first, it is the children who benefit from the successful pitch.

## New Ideas for Children's Programs

Parents and children may not always be at the library, but they are somewhere. Once you determine where they are, pack your story-time bags and go there.

### Parents' Programs

Offering parents' programs does not mean providing informational workshops or programs to parents or caregivers. Rather, what if the library provided support to organizations that have adults-only meetings? During the adults-only program, whether it is at city hall or in your library, the youth services staff would be able to provide a concurrent program for children of the parents or adults attending. When deciding whether to attend such a meeting, parents or caregivers consider the cost of hiring a babysitter and whether it will be worth it. If the library provided this service, the children would have an age-appropriate and educational activity to engage in, and the adults would always remember that the library helped them out. Libraries are not babysitters, and unlike schools, they do not act in loco parentis. Some library districts would find reasons for not providing this service, such as liability or the excessive cost of staff time.

If your library provides community meeting rooms, you are already doing this, as the children of the participating adults trickle in and out of the children's room, largely unattended, during the length of the program. But it's different, you say? Not really.

## Department of Motor Vehicles

The last time you visited the Department of Motor Vehicles (DMV), how many children did you see or hear? Probably more than you expected. Moreover, they are a captive audience. They can't go anywhere until their parents are finished with their business. What a great place to hold story times! These children who would otherwise have to sit still for up to two hours can now be engaged in an educational and fun activity. Convincing the DMV authorities would be the hardest part of this marketing effort, but using phrases such as "You will see fewer children running around" or "There will be less crying and screaming for the hour we are here," you will probably capture the admiration of all DMV employees who have to suffer through these noises daily.

## Shopping Malls/Grocery Stores

Even in the middle of the day, there are children shopping with one or both parents. Malls pride themselves on being family friendly. They have not only stores to purchase your wares but also food courts and carousels, and some even have drop-in babysitting centers. Malls have recognized the needs of parents. Grocery stores are catching on fast, with drop-in child care in the store. Providing a story time at a local mall or grocery store gives parents a bit of a reprieve when shopping with their children, especially during busy holiday seasons. Libraries can provide this respite, even if only for twenty minutes. This service will end up meeting goals of two distinct organizations, the library and the retail management of the mall or grocery chain, as the parents who attend will be grateful to both for providing this unique activity.

## Cultural Events

Most communities, both urban and rural, have cultural events throughout the year. Library districts are beginning to participate more and more in these events but still have not entirely incorporated their services while there. Oftentimes, libraries will have a booth to give out information about their services, but rarely do you see the services in action. Youth services staff, especially, have begun developing culturally diverse materials for their in-house programs, whether to comply with a district multicultural initiative or to meet the needs of their communities. These already developed resources can be displayed at cultural events through a scheduled story time, puppet show, or storytelling session.

## Doctors' Offices

Many pediatricians and family medical practices schedule drop-in hours, a time reserved for parents who were unable to make an appointment for their suddenly ailing child. This is a great place for a story time! Depending on how busy the office is at this time, and waiting rooms are almost always filled, you will be able to reach at least five children and families with your message of education. Parents will not only thank you but they will be more apt to visit that doctor's office in the future, knowing there is something more than the usual ripped books and germ-filled activity gyms for the children to play with. These programs can also be scheduled at traditionally busy times for doctors, such as fall or spring annual physical days.

In virtually every pediatrician's office you find books, magazines, a television, and other activities to occupy the patients while they wait to be called into the examination room. You also find plenty of literature holders throughout the office and exam rooms meant to hold information on the newest prescription drugs available. Although parents do read this information, it may simply be because of lack of choices. Visit doctors in your area and drop off some library literature. Create an activity book or just a simple brochure with information about the library.

When children leave the doctor's office, they are often rewarded with a sticker. If your library has stickers with its logo and identifying information, consider donating bunches of them to the doctors' offices. Doctors will save money on their sticker purchases, and you have promoted your library.

## Community Holiday Observances or Traditions

Every December, no matter where you live, there is a man named Santa whom many children and parents wait in line to see. They hope that after the long wait they will have a special Santa picture to share with family and friends. These lines are grueling, especially with children in tow. Partner with Santa's elves to bring story times to the line. Do the same when the Easter Bunny visits.

Your community may pride itself on its parade traditions. Library districts across the country are being invited to participate in parades and are thinking up unique ways of expressing who librarians are. Wouldn't it be great if the library offered to be the preparade show, in conjunction with the traditional clown posse, and tossed out library promotional materials? Maybe this same staff would just sit down and do an impromptu story time for a group of anxious and antsy children. One book is all you would need. Read it, give them something to remember you by, and move on down the road.

## Birthday Parties

Many successful outreach librarians who focus on offering traditional library programs such as puppet shows, storytelling, and audience participation songs and stories are asked at least once if they are available for children's birthday parties. Most libraries shy away because they feel the library is education, not entertainment. What a fantastic compliment to be asked! It probably comes from parents who are planning to pay someone to simply paint faces and make balloon characters. Youth services departments are typically equipped with a story room (or some type of separate space within the library where programs are conducted). Make your library available for birthday parties, provide entertainment through puppet shows, and create an environment where kids can come back to with pleasant memories. Don't want to host the event? Send your outreach staff to the home or park where the birthday party is taking place. This is the perfect place to distribute stickers, pencils, or whatever marketing items your library offers. Invest in "I had a birthday; READ all about it" T-shirts, and give one to each partygoer. Set limits on the number of kids and length of time. Provide this as a free service. If parents want to pay you anyway, ask them to make a donation to the library or your library friends group instead. If you wonder how this is relevant to library services, it is roughly equivalent to the monthly story time that libraries do for the "Mommy and Me" or church groups.

## Other Locations

There are many other places where children could be reached: local health clubs, day spas, banks, grocery stores, coffee shops, and children's furniture stores. Providing services to all of these places may at first seem overwhelming. It is important to keep in mind the goals of the library organization, including any age-specific priorities, as well as the goals of your marketing plan.

# Chapter Four

# Online Outreach

**W**hen it comes to marketing trends, one thing is clear: marketing online is quickly becoming the preferred tactic. Many articles, books, and websites are devoted to creating, evaluating, and maintaining a library web presence. Fewer, though, are guides and manuals to help librarians learn how to use their websites in a nontraditional way. The standard-issue library website states library hours and locations, provides information on how to use the catalog and reserve a book, offers links to electronic proprietary resources such as databases and indexes, and normally has a "contact-us" section, which may or may not list an e-mail contact. But how best to reach and retain that very important set of patrons—children—via the Web?

Retail marketing has always segmented its population, or customer base, and directed the information to its preferred audience—that is, those most likely to purchase—and this remains important in both libraries and online marketing. Libraries are more like retail shops than we like to accept. When you walk into a retail store, you have choices to make and separate departments to visit based on your needs. Staff in the departments that you visit are specially trained in the products being sold or provided, in both retail stores and libraries. If you are looking for homework help in the library, you will visit the children's department, just as you would shop in the children's area in a department store when looking for children's clothes. And if children go "shopping" in the library—especially via the Internet—the library must be child friendly, in many ways.

When using your library website to reach children, it is of the utmost importance that the language used is understandable by the students you wish to reach. Naming a section *Reference* on a children's library web page that hopes to reach third through sixth graders may seem like a noble idea. After all, it is our job as librarians to empower everyone to use the correct terms for the sections in our library, and who else is going to do it if we don't? Instead of *Reference*, however, try *Homework*. For school-age kids, these two words mean the same thing. Before entering the library profession, had you ever picked up an encyclopedia just because it looked interesting? You probably used it to look up something for school, the same way kids today use it. If you are in youth services, then you understand the nonfiction-versus-reference quandary. Students often arrive at the library armed with knowledge from their teachers and parents and prepared to do a report on some subject or another. As they approach the desk, you see the intent in their eyes—they are empowered—and they speak: "I need to check out a reference book on . . ." Our heads spin, and we respond as rationally as we can with "Do you mean a nonfiction book?" Of course they do! But instead of taking the opportunity to educate them on the difference between the two types of books, we have turned them off to the library, our staff, and our services because we took away all of the power they had when they walked in. Using the word *Reference* on your website is the same. Organizing the children's section of your website requires you to think like a kid. If you will be programming online for children, you must do the same.

## Is the Website Outreach?

*Outreach* is defined as leaving the traditional library setting and providing services to specialized communities at their locations. The library website can be seen as either an extension of services or sometimes as another branch in the library district. Although these are both somewhat accurate, in truth, through the website, the number of reachable patrons is much greater than the potential for each branch individually. In addition, the website serves the entire community rather than designated subsections that are assigned to each branch. Your virtual, or online, library staff is your primary outreach team. Most likely, all outreach efforts point potential users to this specific location for one reason: they don't have to leave their homes to receive library services. For children, the ability to reach a librarian online is absolutely necessary. They are natural-born virtual users. This is their technology. What kinds of products should librarians offer these savvy customers?

ONLINE LIBRARY PRODUCTS

Libraries around the globe are offering access to resources that were previously available only *in* the library. Library patrons are able to access a full range of traditional services with a valid library card and Internet access. In addition to the 24/7 support of virtual librarians, libraries offer a vast array of online products.

> *Informational*, including library locations and hours and library card applications
>
> *Reference*, including authoritative electronic encyclopedias, dictionaries, and databases with full-text articles
>
> *Readers' Advisory*, including subscription-based readers' advisory resources
>
> *Circulation*, including library catalog access, account access, and request and renewal of materials

Each of these items has definite kid appeal, especially in mid-May, when students are given their last chance to complete their homework assignments for the year. As a librarian, however, you must notice that there is one *major* function of public libraries that is missing, and that is the tradition of children's programming.

# Online Programming

Libraries are engaging in more and more online programming through their websites. Online library programming can be put into two categories: group and individual. All online library programs remove one of the most common barriers to using the library—transportation to and from the library.

## Group Programming

In the group online program, kids are actively involved in an online group activity at the same time as other children, and the program is directed by an online library staff member, who serves as a moderator. Group programs would be most similar to existing in-house library programs where there is a scheduled time, specific age group, and detailed outline of events. Probably the most used active programming takes place in the form of online author, artist, and celebrity chats.

### ONLINE CHATS

Most libraries are unable to host author visits because they are so cost prohibitive, and the attendance may not be large enough to support the budget request. Yet many authors, artists, and other famous people are happy to be scheduled for an online chat at a very reduced rate—and sometimes for free. Contact the specific author or artist for his or her fee schedule. Even if this online event is scheduled during school hours, students will participate only if they and their teachers know about it. Not only can online chats save the library time and increase program attendance but they also dispel many a stereotype about librarians as being unhip and increase the coolness factor of the library. Kids will be talking about the library more than ever and probably asking each other, "Do librarians know how to chat?"

Group programs also include online book clubs for children, with a set meeting date and time, or an online scavenger hunt (see below) with a race component. With the advances in technology and the creativity of librarians, online group programming is sure to expand.

## Individual Programming

Individual online library programming is available for children any time they want, from any location, via the library website. More than one child is able to participate at the same time, but the activity is created to meet any personal time constraints and educational needs. Individual online programs can be turned into group activities, especially in a classroom setting, whereas group programs would fall flat if used as individual programs. Because traditional library programs sustain themselves through larger attendance numbers, individual programming in libraries has been almost restricted to the reference transaction. Yet numerous online activities are targeted to the individual user.

## SCAVENGER HUNTS

Think back to when the cool third-grade teacher, the one you didn't have, gave his class the assignment to complete a scavenger hunt. Your friends who were in his class were so excited that they were able to find things on the list that it made your "read-and-recite" homework seem more boring than ever. How you wished you could be in that class! Little did those students know that their teacher was quite creative, and they were actually learning while having fun. Libraries can learn from this. Whether you call it a scavenger hunt or create an "Internet Detectives" or "Library Detectives" group with special incentives, whatever you do, make it edutainment. Make this an empowering exercise for students to learn how to effectively use the library and all its resources.

## EDUCATIONAL GAMES

Libraries rent out commercial CD-ROM software, which should be reviewed as carefully as other materials are in the library. And this material circulates more than traditionalists would like it to. Computer games are what kids look for when checking out online sites, and although suitable games may be purchased, many libraries create their own games. When creating an online game, as with the scavenger-hunt concept, make the game both educational and entertaining. It will take a team of people to create the materials, to compile the resources, and to test its capabilities. The Web on Wheels program of the Las Vegas–Clark County Library District utilizes a web game that can only be accessed by students who attended one of the outreach events. The special password is announced during the event, and children are challenged to remember it to access the games.

Defining the extent of the game, including its grade level, and using up-to-date technology are important. Once implemented, these games can reside on the library website for as long as you wish.

## STORY TIMES

The Public Library of Charlotte and Mecklenburg County revolutionized story times when it began its StoryPlace for children. In the

"About" section of the StoryPlace website, the history and philosophy of the site are unveiled.

> Children and their parents have for years enjoyed attending story times, checking out books and participating in a number of other educational, entertaining and participatory programs at the various locations of The Public Library of Charlotte and Mecklenburg County. StoryPlace, an interactive web site, came about to provide children with the virtual experience of going to the library and participating in the same types of activities the library offers. In the summer of 1999, a team of Children's Librarians and Specialists got together with in-house web developers to begin development on this exciting site. In the spring of 2000, StoryPlace premiered with its first section, the Pre-School Library, completed.[1]

Realizing the potential of electronic resources, and the value of children as users, the library successfully continues this service. Each online story is accompanied by an online activity, take-home activity, and a reading list pertaining to the theme of the story. The ideas and organization presented are the same ideas and organization used in physical preschool story times.

In many instances, librarians provide theme-based programming with an activity component and offer book displays on the same theme in the story room. The stories are already chosen, the activity decided on, and the reading list compiled from the library's live, in-house program. Thus, pulling this together would not mean creating materials from scratch, except for the original story on the theme, but rather taking a successful, educational, and captivating existing story time and putting it online. Libraries offer reference service 24/7; why not story times, too?

## ART EXHIBITIONS

Many libraries are associated with local art agencies or museums through physical sharing of space, allowing artwork to be displayed in libraries or hosting formal art exhibitions for a limited time. Although there are some intricacies to work out for an online art exhibit, if your library is already involved in this realm, these details will be easy to distinguish. In a physical library where artwork is displayed, there is normally a title and short explanation of the piece placed near the artwork. This can easily be transferred online. Most large art museums rent out headsets with information on the works to be looked at that can be worn as the patron tours the exhibit. Why not incorporate this into an online exhibit? Most school library and classroom computers come equipped with headsets (or they can be borrowed). Through your partnerships with your schools, talk with the art teachers, encourage them to have their students tour an exhibit online, and have a fantastic list of resources available for students looking for more information.

Not all libraries will be able to present extensive online programming, but keep these simple, time-saving tips in mind.

> *There is no reason to create something new for online use.* Use existing story-time materials and reach a much broader audience.
>
> *Think like a kid.* Use colors, themes, and fonts that children find appealing. If you are not sure that your idea is the same as theirs, ask them.
>
> *Highlight what the library can do for its younger users.* Use phrases such as "You can access . . ." or "You will find . . ." rather than "The library gives you access . . ." or "The library has this resource to help you find . . ." Using child-centered language will empower the students to continue using their library.

Whether you choose to use your website for outreach or to physically visit populations outside of your library walls, you will need to be involved in actively selling your service. Chapter 5 will guide you through that process.

NOTE

1. Public Library of Charlotte and Mecklenburg County, StoryPlace. Available from http://www.storyplace.org/about.asp.

# Chapter Five

# Selling Your Service

Through creating a marketing and outreach plan, your library district has recognized the benefits of outreach to children. A budget has been delineated and staffing acknowledged. Before implementing the plan and moving into the contact phase, be sure the following budgetary and staffing objectives are met.

## Program Budget

Creating a program budget, instead of a line-item budget, works better for libraries, according to Darlene Weingand, in her book *Marketing/Planning Library and Information Services*:

> Municipalities and institutions frequently have definite requirements concerning the format to be submitted. Such conformity is understandable from the funding authority's point of view because it makes the task of comparison of budget requests from multiple units an easier exercise. However, the standard format, which is commonly the *line item budget*, may be less effective from the information agency's planning perspective. Whatever the official requirement, developing *a program budget* meshes logically with the process of identifying cost factors for each library product.

Program budgeting allows the total agency budget to be constructed program by program. By allocating all debits and credits to individual products, it becomes a relatively simple matter to defend a budget in like manner: program by program. Whereas it is a rather clinical, objective exercise for a funding authority to manage a 3 percent cut in an overall budget or perhaps in a particular budget category, it is much more graphic—and difficult—to face the possible elimination of a well-recognized, effective program.[1]

In essence, your program, no matter how large or small, should have its own budget. Knowing exactly what the cost is for administering this particular program will better define the program. The program budget should be made available to all those directly affected by it, which includes any people involved in the outreach team or effort.

In addition to developing a concrete budget for the program, the library must also establish procedures for who is able to access those funds and the process for retrieving them. Oftentimes, budgets are created, kept, and administered by someone uninvolved in the process. The process of accessing budgetary funds is quite time-consuming, and many times those submitting budget requests are led through lines of red tape. Understandably, the library needs to have some measures of accountability, but, unfortunately, many of the people signing off on the requests are not entrenched in the program. What freedom your outreach team leader will feel when he or she is presented with a program budget along with the procedure for procuring and expending those funds! Give that person the responsibility of maintaining the budget, and he or she will not only have a vested interest in ensuring that the budget is adhered to but will understand that he or she has the ultimate decision-making power and will be held responsible for supporting any requests. Having too many layers of signatures not only slows down the process of using dedicated funds but it also allows for each of the signers to give his or her input and personal opinions about what is being spent, which may cause some to reconsider signing the form. If your outreach team is considered as separate dedicated staff, then their budget should be treated the same way as other departmental budgets. Expenditures from existing budgets should need no more than three signatures before the funds are released: first, the outreach team leader; second, the administrator in charge of outreach; and, finally, the finance office.

## Program Staff

When determining the need of staffing for outreach efforts, consider staff numbers, schedules, and abilities. Whatever type of team you create, your staffing needs should already be included in the program budget. If not, you need to reevaluate the budget. Without staff there cannot be service.

### Staff Numbers

How many staff members are needed to effectively implement a program will be determined more concretely as the program is evaluated, but when starting a program, defining the staff size is imperative. Whether your district decides to create a specific team of outreach specialists or to use existing branch staff on a rotating basis, there needs to be at least one full-time manager of the outreach effort. This outreach services manager will be responsible for scheduling both staff and services, keeping statistics and other records, and acting as the community liaison. In addition to administrative duties, this staff member will be primarily responsible for preparing and presenting outreach presentations. That is a huge workload for one person and will most definitely lead to early and quick burnout and apathy from that librarian. Rather than risk losing a good leader, hire a team of outreach specialists to work with each other and community agencies.

This outreach team can be as small as two full-time employees and as large as can be supported by community response and budgetary restraints. By creating a devoted outreach team, the library shows its support for the program as well as acknowledges that outreach, as an added duty to an existing position, may cause a high turnover rate among creative and energetic staff. If your district cannot afford a devoted team, other options include regularly scheduling existing staff on a rotating schedule or mandating that each branch staff member attend one outreach event per year (or other specific time frame). Whatever method is chosen, all staff directly involved need to know each other's strengths and weaknesses and be able to work as a team.

### Staff Schedules

Outreach can happen any place and any time. Although it would be ideal if staff were equally as available, it is not good internal customer service. Staff should be flexible but not overwhelmed. We all know that outreach can be exhausting, whether promoting summer reading programs or sitting at a booth at a community event. With staff exhaustion comes reduced quality of service.

Creating a set schedule for your full-time outreach staff (for example, five days on, followed by two days off) is the best option. When starting any new program, many libraries want to make it work, whatever the cost. Yet the cost of losing highly qualified outreach specialists cannot be counted in strict monetary numbers. The five-day workweek is common in most libraries for nonoutreach staff, yet it is not uncommon to see outreach staff working strange schedules to accommodate all outreach events. Look at your marketing plan and determine where your outreach will most likely be conducted, and structure your full-time employees' schedules accordingly. If the goal is to reach school-age children at school, and school hours are from 8 a.m. to 3 p.m., Monday through Friday, schedule your staff from 7 a.m. to 4 p.m., Monday through Friday. This will give them enough time to prepare for the presentations and allow a more flexible scheduling of presentations. If your goal is to reach children at after-school sites, and those agency hours are from 10 a.m. to 6 p.m., Tuesday through Saturday, schedule your staff from 9 a.m. to 7 p.m., Tuesday through Saturday. If your goal is to be available for all community events that take place on the weekends, schedule your full-time staff regularly for those days. Your full-time staff schedules should closely relate to the schedules of the children you are intent on reaching. Part-time staff schedules should be created in the same manner. Creating set schedules allows outreach staff plenty of off time to recoup from a hard week of outreach and to come to work refreshed after a two-day break.

## Staff Abilities

Hiring staff for a team of outreach specialists requires more attention to detail and focus than simply hiring a children's librarian. Although certain skill sets are required to be a successful youth services librarian, librarians can learn most of those skills, such as reference and collection development, on the job. All applicants should be aware of what is expected of them, including any special skills that may be required. The library human resources professional can help determine the best verbiage for the job descriptions, but the following qualities ought to be required in any youth outreach position.

## CREATIVITY

Staff must not only appreciate good works of literature but also be able to express that appreciation to children. To be successful, staffers need to be creative in both expression and thought.

## FLEXIBILITY

Because of the possibly changing nature of the program, staff hired need to be flexible enough in thought to let go of ideas that aren't working and to think of new ideas to try. Staff must understand that change is the only constant in an outreach program and that program changes should not be taken personally.

## ORGANIZATION

Outreach programs will most likely receive some if not all of their funds from external agencies. To show these agencies that the funds were used resourcefully and productively, all outreach staff need to be able to organize both statistics and thoughts and report clearly on them. In addition, the more organized the effort, the more successful it will be.

## PUBLIC SPEAKING

Public speaking is not a skill people can learn overnight. New staff who are afraid of being the center of attention or of standing in front of large groups of people will probably need more training in the art of public speaking than outreach.

Any intelligent and enthusiastic person hired as an outreach specialist can learn the other skills needed to make the program a success, such as implementing library policy, storytelling, puppeteering, and managing a classroom or a crowd. Although applicants should certainly be asked about the level of skill they have in these areas, library districts should be most concerned with their creativity, flexibility, and organizational and public-speaking abilities.

## Implementing the Plan

Once outreach staff are hired and the budget is clearly in place, it is time to implement the plan. Using the market analysis and planning stage, staff should have already begun compiling lists of community agencies to contact. With so much technology available, keeping these lists can be as simple as creating a new address book in one of your available computer programs or using a contact sheet, such as the one show in figure 5.1, that lists the agency's name; phone number; address; website; mission statement, vision statement, and service area; and contact name. This information should be kept on every entity contacted. Keep all of your contacts in one place, whether it is on the computer or on paper. This list will be where you start when selling your services.

Simple reference resources such as the local phone book or agency websites will give you the information you need to create useful contact lists. Prior to making contact, review any content about the agency and note it in your file. If you are still unclear, be sure to have them clarify when you contact them. If your plan is to work specifically with schools, keep a separate contact sheet for each school.

Partnering with schools requires a more detailed contact sheet. Although contacting the school librarian first seems to be the plan for

| Agency |
|---|
| Phone |
| Address |
| Website |
| Mission/Vision/Service Area |
| Contact Name |

**Figure 5.1**  *Sample Contact Sheet*

most libraries, should this contact not result in successful promotion, you ought to have a list of other possible contacts for the school. Author and consultant Patrick Jones (http://www.connectingya.com) has developed a "Sample School Planning Document" for this school and public library partnership (see figure 5.2).[2] This form is useful, especially when staff present subject- or theme-based programs or when the first contact with the school fails.

## First Contact

Once you have a relatively complete list of agencies to contact, prepare and send a letter about your program. When addressing the letter, use specific contact information such as the name of the director, librarian, or teacher. This letter should be informative, to the point, and upbeat. Remember that the adults you are trying to contact are also being contacted by other agencies selling a service or product. S. R. Ranganathan, the great Indian library theorist, states in his fourth law of library science, "Save the time of the reader." Use this law when sending any written correspondence about your new service or program. Make your letter stand out by printing it on library letterhead, including the library logo in a prominent place, and getting to the point quickly. See figure 5.3 for an example of a good first-contact letter.

If letters aren't your thing, try sending a promotional flyer that can double as a mailer. This will be more expensive than a simple letter but may produce better results because of its graphic nature. The Las Vegas–Clark County Library District used this format in promoting its new Web on Wheels program in 2001, as seen in figure 5.4.

After you have mailed the letter, note the date and type of contact on your follow-up sheet (figure 5.5 shows a sample follow-up sheet). It is important to keep track of your contact information as specifically as possible. This follow-up sheet should be kept close to the outreach department phone for easy access during incoming and outgoing phone calls. If your outreach department has its own desktop computer, you may choose to keep all of this information in a file on that computer. If your department has only a laptop for staff use, you might want to have a hard copy available and to input the new, written information on a regular basis. This updated file should be printed and kept near the phone.

| Name of School | | | |
|---|---|---|---|
| Address | | | |
| Primary Phone # | | | |
| Fax Number | | | |
| Web Page | | | |
| School District | | | |

## Key Contacts

| TITLE | NAME | PHONE | E-MAIL |
|---|---|---|---|
| Art Dept. Chair | | | |
| Athletic Dept. Chair | | | |
| English Dept. Chair | | | |
| Guidance Dept. Chair | | | |
| Head Librarian | | | |
| Principal | | | |
| PTO Newsletter Editor | | | |
| PTO President | | | |
| School Newsletter Editor | | | |
| School Paper Advisor | | | |
| School Secretary | | | |
| Security Chief | | | |
| Service Learning Chair | | | |

**FIGURE 5.2**  *Sample School Planning Document*

| TITLE | NAME | PHONE | E-MAIL |
|---|---|---|---|
| Technology Dept. Chair | | | |
| Theater Dept. Chair | | | |
| Other | | | |

## Key Documents

| DOCUMENT | CONTACT | OBTAIN? |
|---|---|---|
| AR and other reading lists | | |
| Bell schedule | | |
| Club or organization list | | |
| Curriculum guide | | |
| Library guides, pathfinders, etc. | | |
| PTO newsletter subscription | | |
| School calendar | | |
| School newsletter subscription | | |
| School newspaper subscription | | |
| Student handbook | | |
| Teacher roster | | |
| Yearbook | | |
| Other | | |

LIBRARY LOGO


Library Address
Library WebSite
Library Phone Number

Date

Contact Name
Contact Agency
Contact Address

Dear Contact Name,

Your library has always been a source of informational and curricular materials for both you and your students. We have expanded our services to include free presentations to students, in your school or classroom, on common topics and themes. Our presentations are approximately thirty minutes in length, and will be tailored to accommodate the specific grade level of the participating students. More information about our services can be found at our website: INSERT WEB ADDRESS.

We have limited dates available for the remainder of the year. Call us directly at 555-1212 to schedule a free library presentation for your students or if you have any questions about our service.

We look forward to hearing from you.

Sincerely,


NAME
Library District Outreach Department

**Figure 5.3** *First-Contact Letter Example*


Do not be discouraged if your letters receive no immediate response. Educators receive a lot of promotional materials and often keep a file of people to contact for special events. It is very likely that your letter

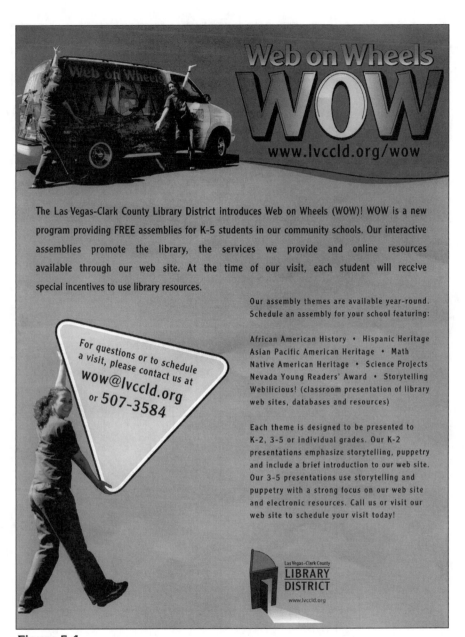

**Figure 5.4**

was received and is on their to-do list. Approximately seven to ten business days after sending the letters, if you still have not received a response, prepare to begin calling.

| Agency Name | Contact Name | Phone Number | Date Contacted | Contact Type/ Result | Date Contacted | Contact Type/ Result | Date Contacted | Contact Type/ Result |
|---|---|---|---|---|---|---|---|---|
| | | | | | | | | |
| | | | | | | | | |
| | | | | | | | | |
| | | | | | | | | |
| | | | | | | | | |
| | | | | | | | | |
| | | | | | | | | |
| | | | | | | | | |
| | | | | | | | | |
| | | | | | | | | |
| | | | | | | | | |
| | | | | | | | | |
| | | | | | | | | |
| | | | | | | | | |
| | | | | | | | | |
| | | | | | | | | |

**Figure 5.5** *Sample Follow-Up Sheet*

## Second Contact

Your second contact with community agencies will either come from the agency contacting you as a result of the letter received or you contacting the agency via telephone to follow up on the letter you sent. Either way, ensure that all types of contact are noted on the follow-up sheet.

### MAKING CONTACT

When calling an agency, keep it simple and keep it brief (about five to ten minutes). Standard phone etiquette applies (for example, speak clearly and politely), as do some selling techniques (for example, enthusiastically describe your services and encourage the agency to schedule a visit). Using a script when calling works for many (see box 5.1 for a sample phone script), but scripted phone calls frequently sound too rehearsed, so take care to keep an element of spontaneity in your call. Another option is to use an outline of what you will say when you speak with your contact to help standardize the process. The outline does not need to be read verbatim, but it should contain all of the items you would like to mention. When calling, have a smile on your face; it will come across in your tone of voice. Ask if your contact is available. If yes, ask to be transferred if it is not offered.

When your contact arrives on the line, use the following outline:

> *Begin the call*
>> Introduce yourself
>> Identify your agency
>> State the purpose of your call
>> Describe your services
>> Encourage visit scheduling

> *End the call*
>> Repeat your name and agency name
>> Give contact information
>> Restate visit date and time
>> Update your visit calendar

**Box 5.1** *Sample Phone Script*

| | |
|---|---|
| *Introduce yourself* | Hi, _____.<br>CONTACT NAME<br><br>My name is _____.<br>NAME |
| *Identify agency* | I am with the _____,<br>LIBRARY DISTRICT NAME<br><br>in the _____.<br>DEPARTMENT NAME |
| *Purpose of call* | We are offering a *free* service to students in our community.<br>    Our multicultural, theme-based assemblies are appropriate for grades K-2 and 3–5. Our unique presentations use a mix of technology and storytelling and have been designed to meet diversity and literacy curriculum fundamentals. These assemblies will encourage cultural literacy, as well as information literacy, and promote the use of the public library. All of our presentations are delivered at your school so there is no need to arrange transportation. |
| *Encourage visit scheduling* | The presentations last 30 to 45 minutes and can be scheduled at a time most convenient for your students. We have limited dates available for the remainder of the year.<br><br>Do you have any questions before we schedule your visit? |

Be sure to have your outreach schedule and calendar ready for scheduling. Items to be kept on this departmental calendar include existing obligations and staff schedules. Keep your calendar ready at all times, both on and off the road. You may want to keep this calendar very close to the follow-up sheet for your department as these two documents go hand in hand.

## LEAVING A MESSAGE

If your contact is not available when you call, ask if you can leave a message (see box 5.2 for a sample phone message). Whether you are leaving a message with a person or on your contact's voice mail, it is important to be clear and concise. Messages that are too long risk being ignored by the listener or cut off by the voice-mail system. When you leave a message with a person, identify yourself and your agency, state the purpose of the call, and leave your phone number. When you leave a message on voice mail, follow the same steps but be more descriptive about the purpose of the call and state your name and phone number twice. A response should be encouraged.

## Third Contact

If a third contact is needed, repeat the "Second Contact" procedure, but wait at least two work weeks before the third contact. If you call the Monday before a holiday break or closure, wait until a week after the agency reopens to call back. When making the third call, if your contact is still not available, ask the secretary about the best time to reach your contact. Also, try calling on a different day of the week. Because you have been keeping track of all contacts on the follow-up sheet, you can easily ascertain what day you previously called.

Your third contact may also be a return phone call from an interested educator as a result of your second contact. If this is the case, be sure to fill in the correct space on the follow-up sheet.

## Fourth and Final Contact

Perhaps you have sent a letter and called at least twice, and you still have not received a response from your contact. The fourth contact phase can be a challenging situation: should you write a letter, make another call, or give up? Some suggest that you end your communication attempts with a letter to your contact person. This letter, like the first contact, will serve as a brief introduction to the services you are offering. Regardless of the frustration you may feel after receiving no response to your communication attempts, be certain that the letter in no way indicates that feeling. Keep it cordial and simple, and, again, save the time of the reader. Instead of saying "We are now

**Box 5.2** *Leaving a Message*

| | |
|---|---|
| *Identify yourself* | My name is _____. <br> NAME |
| *Identify agency* | I am with the _____, <br> LIBRARY DISTRICT NAME <br><br> in the _____. <br> DEPARTMENT NAME |
| *Purpose of call* | *With a Person* <br><br> I am calling to schedule a *free* library presentation for his/her students. <br><br> *Voice Mail* <br><br> I am calling to schedule a *free* library presentation for your students. We have many theme- and curricular-based presentations that will be both educational and entertaining for your students. There is no need to arrange transportation as we come to you. Our services are *free* and can be scheduled at your convenience. |
| *Phone number* | *With a Person* <br><br> I can be contacted directly at: <br><br> _____. <br> PHONE NUMBER <br><br> *Voice Mail* <br><br> Again, my name is <br><br> _____ <br> NAME <br><br> from the _____, <br> LIBRARY DISTRICT NAME <br><br> and I can be reached at: <br><br> _____. <br> PHONE NUMBER <br><br> I look forward to hearing from you. <br><br> Good-bye. |

scheduling for the upcoming school year," promote a sense of urgency and belonging. Use phrases such as "We have limited dates available for the remainder of the year" or "Many of your colleagues have enjoyed our presentations, and we are happy to share their comments with you when you call to schedule your visit." However you phrase it, remember to keep it simple and sincere.

If you insist on calling that contact one last time, instead of leaving another message, ask the secretary if there might be another person who is able to schedule literacy presentations for students. Very often the secretary is the main source of agency information and will be able to direct you to a more responsive person. If this is the case, and a new contact is received, start the entire contact cycle from the "Second Contact" phase.

## Know When to Stop

Contacting potential outreach sites is time-consuming, but if successful contact is made, your program will also be successful. Unlike telemarketers, who really don't stop until they make contact, library marketers need to have a limit. One letter, two phone calls, and a final letter is plenty of admirable effort. If after attempting contact four times you still do not receive a response, you can be assured that the lack of interest is not caused by lack of persistence.

If you have reached the stopping point for contacts and still have goals to reach, this is a great time to evaluate the program. You will need to change your focus and start the communication cycle from the beginning with your newly identified agencies.

The process of communicating with potential clients will last throughout the year or the defined time frame of the project. This is not something that can be done in only a designated month, nor is it something that will come to a close. Scheduling a staff member to perform these duties is an efficient way of handling them. It only takes one person to make contact with the agencies. Set a daily goal of five to ten agencies. Set a time of day that works best for reaching your contacts. When working with schools, after-school programs, and community agencies focused on serving children, call before students arrive for the day. To find out what time that is, ask the receptionist or refer to your agency information sheet. Schedule outreach staff to communicate with potential sites at times that will receive the most direct contacts.

You have successfully sold your service. And who says outreach isn't marketing? Now you need to prepare for the visit as best you can. Chapter 6 takes you through the various stages of preparation for any outreach visit.

## NOTES

1. Darlene Weingand, *Marketing/Planning Library and Information Services*, 2d ed. (Littleton, CO: Libraries Unlimited, 1999), 102.
2. Patrick Jones, "Sample School Planning Document," personal communication with author, July 28, 2004.

# Chapter Six

# Preparing for the Presentation

**Y**ou have visits scheduled. Congratulations! This chapter addresses a few time-saving preparations that can make the presentation both successful and efficient. Your outreach visits should have four separate components: packing, setup, presentation, and breakdown. Mastering each of these components allows you to both save the time of the host agency and to reach more children each day.

## Packing

Much like packing a suitcase to go on vacation, when you pack for an outreach visit, make sure you have all the materials you may need to make a successful presentation. Using a checklist before each event allows you to be very specific about what exactly is needed and ensures that you have all that is needed. Your checklist should be as specific as possible and include *all* of your presentation items. Librarians are only human, and we do forget things. With your checklist in hand, you will forget less. If you have theme programs that require certain materials, create a checklist for each of the presentations as well as a general checklist. As the name states, you will need to check off the materials as they are packed. You may choose to print numerous copies of the checklist, each for a onetime use; use a spreadsheet format that will allow you to check by date; or simply print one checklist, keep it in a page protector, and use a wax pencil for checking off the items. Whichever format you choose, make sure that the checklist contains sections for the following items.

*Equipment*
Computer
Projector
Puppet stage
Sound system
Microphones

*Materials*
Books
Library cards
Library materials

*Props*
Puppets (list each individually)
Backdrops

*Program Information*
Business cards
Evaluation forms
Novelty items

Creating a checklist, and using it before leaving your home base for each program, will give you the assurance that you have what you need. It will not, however, make missing items appear suddenly as you realize you have forgotten them. Using a checklist in your packing phase should not take you more than fifteen minutes, and it is always time well spent.

## Setup

When you arrive at your site, first check in at the office or with your contact person. With heightened security everywhere, be sure you have your library ID as well as another form of photo ID available.

Once you are escorted or directed to the presentation area, scope it out and decide on the best location to set up the show. If you are using a pull-down screen provided by the agency, and it is stationary in one part of the room, you need to be nearest to that. Ask your contact person where the kids will be sitting. It is best to center yourself and the presentation in the middle of a large room, but choose a location where most kids can easily see you and you have access to the outlets, tables, or other host-provided materials you have requested. Be sure the equipment that is supposed to be provided by the agency is in place; if not, ask again to have the equipment available. Your total setup should take no more than thirty minutes for an assembly or large group presentation. Yes, half an hour! In thirty minutes, you should be able to arrive, set up, review the entire presentation, and have time for a five-minute rest before the kids arrive. To reach the thirty-minute goal, practice the entire setup process at your home base until you can meet or beat that timed goal.

## Setup Dress Rehearsal

You know how to set up your program. You have done it in your head and talked about it a million times. Even so, taking the following dress-rehearsal steps will give you a clearer picture of the actual amount of time it will take.

> Pick a location in your library, and be sure it is available for at least an hour. Set a time for your fake presentation, and plan to arrive thirty minutes early.

> Pack up as if you were going to an actual site. Really. Pack everything. Completely disconnect any technology items in use at the outreach office and pack them. Get your puppets, books, and library materials ready. Be sure to use your checklist.

> Arrive at the specified library location thirty minutes before the start of the presentation and begin setting up. Set everything up. Unpack completely. Connect all wires, cables, and power plugs. Set up your puppet stage. Lay out your materials in order to make the presentation more effective and efficient. Review the presentation.

> When you feel setup is complete, look at the clock. If it took
> you longer than thirty minutes, try again. Keep rehears-
> ing until you can meet that thirty-minute goal.

If your presentation will be in a classroom or other small group
setting, you may be setting up while students are still actively working. When this is the case, move quickly and quietly to show respect
for the teacher and allow the students to learn. In the setup phase,
students become quite inquisitive and often begin to not only ask
questions about who you are and what you are going to do but also to
tell you about themselves. Never ignore students who approach you
during setup time. Instead, take time to mimic their enthusiasm and
to listen to what they have to say. If the questions don't cease and are
delaying your setup, simply inform the students of what you need to
do and excuse yourself. These chatty students will be pleased to have
talked to you before the others, and they will probably be your most
attentive participants once you begin.

## Presentation

The actual presentation should be between thirty and forty-five
minutes long. It should be able to be modified when necessary to
accommodate agencies' time restrictions. It should also be adaptable
so that when you are presenting, you have enough leeway to make
time for dealing with behavior problems, seating latecomers, or
reevaluating the comprehension level of the students. During setup,
all items were placed in order to make the presentation more effective and efficient. In the presentation phase, after an item, prop, or
book has been used, it too should be put away or placed in a standard
location to ensure a quick breakdown.

### Presentation Dress Rehearsal

Like the setup dress rehearsal, the presentation dress rehearsal should
take place at a time and location where no actual attendees will be
present. Leave yourself enough time to start over and retry as
needed. Ideally, this dress rehearsal should be done immediately
after the successful setup dress rehearsal so that all of your items are
laid out where they are supposed to be.

Practice everything that would or could be done in this presentation. If possible, have a nonperforming staff member time each section of the presentation.

Present each item fully, including reading the entire book or going through the database thoroughly. This will not only give you an idea of the length of each segment but it is also the best way to present.

Make changes as needed during the dress rehearsal, but go through with your original outline at least once before moving components around. If you do make a change, be sure to start the dress rehearsal again using the new outline.

Take note of items that may be removed for time if needed. Schedule the longer items first, and close with shorter or more flexible routines. Should you look at the clock and notice you have three minutes left, and you have a five-minute story and a two-minute audience participation song to do, be prepared to skip the story. You might even choose to sing a verse from the song "one more time" if you need to.

As you rehearse, put used props in the most convenient place. Whether you carry your items in boxes or plastic totes, it might save time to have those immediately behind you so you can put your props back in their proper location as soon as you are finished with them.

Practice your presentation until it meets both your personal needs and the external needs of the agencies where it will be presented. Evaluate it fully after the dress rehearsal and make necessary changes to the outline. Be sure to practice until you are satisfied with the material presented.

## Guidelines for Effective Outreach Presentations

So you have spent countless hours preparing, planning, and practicing, and you know your presentation inside and out. You might be able to do the entire program without looking at the script. What a fantastic feat! When you are finally presenting, be sure to remember the following guidelines:

When you begin, ask if everyone can see and hear you. The last thing you want is for only the front of the group to benefit from your program. Be sure to make adjustments and ask again. Try not to ask more than twice, though, because students may think the entire presentation is "Can you hear me?"

Make eye contact with the students.

Look to each side of a large group, and be sure to look toward the back of the room. By looking toward the back, all of the students feel as if you are talking to them.

If you were able to get a few names of students before the program started, try to incorporate those into your presentation. Be creative, but never single out one student specifically (many students are uncomfortable in the limelight, especially if it shines only on them).

Smile during the presentation. The entire program will not be made up of character roles, reading, or singing. There will be times when you are able to be you. Be sure to smile, especially when informing your audience of the library's many services and opportunities.

Be excited. After the fourth time you present the same program, your enthusiasm may wane. But keep in mind that these students have not seen the presentation before, and simply because it is new, it is exciting. Also remember that children are quite intuitive and will mimic your response to the materials presented.

Use language that is appealing to children. To be sure you are reaching out successfully, define the resources in the students' terms. Use metaphors to relate any new concepts to words students already know. Finally, ask questions occasionally to make sure students understand. For example, when showing a database to children, you may find yourself talking and demonstrating for ten minutes before realizing they don't quite understand. You may even be asked what a database is after you have finished, but not if you have taken the time to ask them what a database is first!

Appeal to their needs and wants, especially when presenting electronic resources. Students know they need to write a report on a person, but they want to have time to play as well. Tell them about the electronic biography resources the library has, explain in enough detail that they will be able to use these resources effectively and quickly, and close by acknowledging that they will still have time to play because the electronic resources will give them the information they need quicker than a general Internet search.

If you have materials to distribute after the program, which you should, discuss the best way to distribute them with the teacher before the program. If your presentation is for a large group, it's a good idea to enlist help distributing the materials. Let the children know they will receive a handout after the program either from you or their teacher.

Once the presentation is finished, it is time to break down your materials, spruce up the area, and head back to the library.

## Breakdown

Breaking down your materials should take no more than fifteen minutes. The items you used should already be in a transportable state except for any major props or equipment such as puppet stages or computers. As discussed, putting the items away as you finish with them decreases breakdown time. Breakdown should be done as quickly as possible so as not to intrude on more class or instruction time, but even so, everything you brought and set up should be placed in its proper casing. Use your checklist to be sure you have everything you came with.

■ ■ ■ ■ ■

The total amount of time it should take for any presentation, from start to finish, is one and a half hours. If you have two presentations in the same room, then add only the presentation time to the total time. Travel time should always be considered as well. If it normally takes twenty minutes to drive from your library to a site, add that time to the beginning and end of the total time. Here is a visual breakdown:

| | |
|---|---|
| *Travel time:* | twenty minutes |
| *Presentation time:* | one hour and thirty minutes (ninety minutes) |
| *Travel time:* | twenty minutes |
| *Total visit time:* | two hours and ten minutes (one hundred and thirty minutes) |

If you can visit one site in three hours or less, and you typically have eight-hour workdays, you can do two site visits per day and still have time for lunch. When you extend this schedule to weekly programs, your staff have the ability to present at up to ten sites per week. Knowing your daily limit is imperative when scheduling the programs.

Mastering each of the steps in the presentation has many benefits. First, by being efficient in the entire process, you will be able to visit more sites per day. Second, because you know specifically how each phase works, you have the flexibility of making immediate changes to a presentation. Third, although some might disagree, the total presentation time is a recordable statistic when evaluating the outreach effort. The time it takes to do an actual program is valid when justifying why you only reached, for example, six sites per week. Chapter 7 covers the importance of tracking outreach via keeping records and statistics for your program.

*Chapter Seven*

# Tracking Outreach

**A**ccountability is important in every new plan and must be a priority for libraries. Too often, as has been stated before, librarians think that because libraries and the information and services provided are intrinsically rewarding, they need to do nothing but use their storytelling skills in persuading administration, outside funding agencies, and potential community partners that youth services are important. Being accountable for the library's outreach efforts gives you and others the hard facts you need to support the continuation or discontinuation of a program. The marketing process is filled with checks and balances, including the common "How did you hear about us?" question posted on private company websites and asked by employees at retail stores. Restaurant customers are given a similar "How are we doing?" survey via questionnaires on tables. Corporate agencies use this information to revise or regroup existing techniques on a regular basis. There are many statistics a library can keep regarding outreach, and it is important to know which will be most valuable and what purpose they serve.

## Intelligent and Intuitive Statistics

Traditional statistics are typically referred to as either qualitative or quantitative, meaning a summary of quality or numbers, respectively, yet library statistics need to appeal to the psychological balance. These library statistics could be termed intelligent and intuitive. Intelligent statistics have many of the same qualities of quantitative statistics. They should be used for tracking and comparing strictly collected numerical data. Libraries use intelligent statistics all of the time when tracking circulation, library use, and program attendance. The same philosophy of counting should apply to outreach efforts. Intuitive statistics—rather than simply counting the number of people or visits to a library—ask about people's feelings on the presentation. The most common intuitive part of an evaluation is the "Comments" section. Although important to have on all evaluations, these intuitive sections can often be difficult to measure, although they can be easily converted to intelligent statistics. For example, you might decide whether the tone of the comments is positive or negative and count the number (intelligent) of positive and negative comments (intuitive). Finding alternate ways of judging perception is not an easy task but one that needs to be done.

## Evaluating Your Services

Continuous evaluation of the outreach program is the only way to know if it is a success. Internal statistics recorded and compiled by the library represent use of the library and are usually only an intelligent measure of the effect of your efforts. The goal of external evaluations should be to compile meaningful statistics on the perception of the program by the participants. Every librarian providing outreach thinks he or she is offering a valuable service. Unfortunately, our grand self-image sometimes gets in the way of how others actually perceive us. Dr. Phil, the renowned psychologist, frequently states that "there is no reality, only perception." What staff librarians think was a really great program may have been perceived as a huge waste of time by the participants. Knowing exactly how the program was perceived, accepting this input as crucial constructive criticism, and making necessary changes to the program immediately will ensure success.

# External Evaluation

Seeking input from outreach recipients is an external statistic. Before you begin creating and printing evaluation forms, be certain that the information you request is what you need to effectively evaluate the program. Changing the evaluation form midyear will result in incomplete reporting and ineffective evaluation. It can be difficult to determine what questions to ask. Using the "Five *P*s" from chapter 1—people, product, place, promotion, and price—in your evaluation questions as a general guideline will help to evaluate all facets of the program. You certainly do not want to ask too many questions as it might deter the user from completing the form, but at the same time, you don't want to gather too little information, which results in an incomplete picture.

The following tips will help you create both printed evaluation forms and online evaluation forms that can be completed by adults working with children or by children alone.

## Printed Evaluation Forms

### GENERAL FORMATTING TIPS

#### *Adults Working with Children*

The evaluation form should be no longer than one side of an 8 ½ x 11 inch piece of paper.

> Fonts used on the form should be no smaller than 8 points.
>
> Include the library logo or the program logo or both.
>
> Include specific contact information for the program, including name, address, phone, fax, e-mail, and web address.
>
> Standardize the style of the questions. There are many options, including multiple choice, true or false, rating system, yes or no, and fill in the blanks. Choose the one that works best for you and stick with it.
>
> Reserve space either at the end of the form or after each individual question for written comments from the participants.

### Children

Use the information listed above and the information below (although questions will need to be reworded into child-friendly language).

> Include child-friendly images of letters, numbers, books, or other library-related kiddie material.
>
> If your library has a library mascot, include its name or likeness on the printed form.

## GENERAL INFORMATION FIELDS

> Name of participating agency
>
> Date of presentation
>
> Name of presenter(s)
>
> Title of program

## TOPICS TO BE EVALUATED

### People

> Who were the presenters?
>
> Were the presenters knowledgeable?
>
> Did they keep the attention of the children?
>
> Were they easily understood?
>
> Were they helpful in answering your questions?

### Product

> Was the information presented valuable to your students?
>
> Did you know about this resource/service/product before our presentation?
>
> How will you incorporate this information into your classroom?

### Place

> Was the location of the program sufficient to the needs of both students and teachers?
>
> Would you like to schedule a class visit to the library?

*Promotion*

How did you hear about this library program?

Will you tell your friends and colleagues about our program?

Can we send you information on new presentations as they become available?

*Price*

In this section of the form, it is important to restate that this was a free library service. Mentioning cost in any way, either by asking "Would you pay for this presentation?" or any other phrasing, will certainly give the wrong impression. A simple statement will do the trick.

> The library strives to provide *free*, high-quality services to children. We appreciate your taking the time to complete this form and return it to the address listed. Doing so will help us to make needed changes so that our program is most effective. Thank you for supporting your library. Together we will make a difference for all children.

Before the closing statement, allow some space for general written comments from the educators. Although these results are difficult to measure, they will provide you with fantastic ideas to incorporate, boost your staff's self-esteem, and give you awesome quotes to use in your reports.

## Online Evaluation Forms

Like printed evaluation forms, there should be one for adults and one for children. Using the same content, or even simply making your printed form accessible online, will result in more coherent statistics. Because it is a different medium, there are additional tips to consider.

### GENERAL FORMATTING TIPS

*Adults Working with Children*

Use the same guidelines as the print format but note the following.

> The form should be interactive and not require printing to complete and submit it, although an option to print should be offered.

If possible, when a patron submits the form electronically, completed forms should be forwarded to an e-mail account that is accessible by all involved parties rather than a personal e-mail. It would be even better if the forms were created in a web database that would keep track of all submitted responses electronically, although software and support for this type of resource can become expensive.

Once the form is submitted, an automatically generated e-mail reply should thank the customer for the support of the library, confirm that the survey was received, and redirect him or her back to the library website.

### Children

Use the information listed above and the information below.

In the thank-you screen, specifically redirect the student to the kids section of the website or offer a relevant homework help tip.

If possible, the online children's evaluation form should feature graphic representation of required answers, such as a smiley face for a yes answer and a sad face for a no answer.

Remember that all children's forms should be written in child-friendly language.

## Distributing Evaluation Forms

If you use printed evaluation forms, be sure to bring enough copies for each of the participants. You can risk giving each site a master copy for your contact person to photocopy and distribute, but you may only receive one form back. Schools, community agencies, day-care centers, and preschools face reduced budgets as much as publicly funded libraries do. Make it easier on the site coordinator by providing him or her with as many copies as you want to receive back. If you want them to send you the completed forms, provide a self-addressed, stamped envelope to send them back in. If you want to receive them by fax, be certain your fax machine is filled with paper and turned on at all times. If you want the forms completed immediately after your program and before you leave the site, bring enough pencils or pens for everyone to use. These pencils may even be printed with your contact information and left at the school as a constant reminder of the program.

If you plan to use online forms, give the direct address to the potential evaluators by distributing any of your marketing materials that have the specific web address or by creating special materials to meet this need. Some adults are wary of submitting information entirely online. Providing each site with a master print copy even when online submission is preferred is a wise move. By doing this, you give them a choice, which is valuable in itself.

The Multnomah County Library School Corps makes it easy for participants in its programs to evaluate its services. Evaluation forms—specific to the various types of presentations—are found on its website (http://www.multcolib.org/schoolcorps) (see figure 7.1). These online forms allow participants to fill in the information and submit

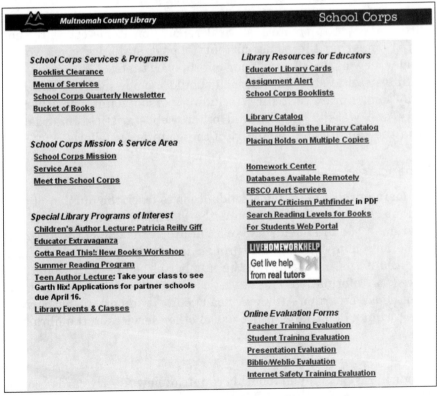

**Figure 7.1**

it online. The forms are easy to read and can be completed quickly, yet they contain valuable evaluative information for the School Corps.

Each of the forms is completed and submitted entirely online. The questions are clear, concise, and valuable. With these forms, the School Corps can keep track of responses to different programs and sort them by type of participant.

## Internal Statistics

The majority of the internal statistics will be intelligent statistics, numbers conveying use of the library. When managing internal statistics, first investigate what reporting mechanisms are already available as well as those currently in use. In a large library district, it may be difficult, if not impossible, to keep accurate manual statistics. When deciding what statistics to keep to track your outreach success, know what statistics are already being kept and whether it will be possible to create historical reports on items currently not kept. Comparing the same current to past statistics gives you a broader view of the effect of your efforts over time.

Internet statistics for outreach should include many of the commonly kept library statistics, including person counts, new library cards, and website visitors and other web statistics. Information about the validity and reliability of these statistics follows.

### Attendance

The main purpose of taking attendance is to track the number of participants. Take a minute to count the attendees at the start of the program. If you are inclined, take a minute at the end of the program to see how many people sat through the entire presentation. This head count will only give you the number of bodies with whom you shared the information. This statistic is like taking the attendance at an in-house program. Although head count is important for current use, it cannot determine future use of other services in the library.

### New Library Cards

If your library has taken monthly counts of new library cards issued, it is best to continue in this fashion. You can compare the number with past statistics. Because there will always be naysayers who attribute an increase to everything but outreach efforts, keeping specific statistics is important. For example, if your library district has five branch libraries and one main library and each library is responsible for certain zip-code or other predetermined demographic areas, note that same information for where the outreach event took place. When running the monthly report for new library cards, delineate it by zip code (or other demographic indicators). If your monthly outreach events took place in zip codes 12345 and 23456, compare the usual number of new library cards in those zip codes to the current monthly statistics. If there is a greater number and there were no other unusual circumstances, such as an increase in in-house library programs, it is safe to say that outreach increased the number of new library cards issued.

If you would rather count the specific number of outreach-related new library cards, you can do it either electronically or manually. If your automation system allows you to run reports by library card type, then creating a special code for cards issued as a result of outreach will help. Adding a code such as "JO" (for Juvenile Outreach) or "YO" (for Youth Outreach) to the list of available card or patron types will make this reporting easier. For it to be successful, however, all staff who register new users will need to be made aware of this new card type and know exactly when to use it. Outreach staff should always distribute library card applications, and often they are exactly the same as those distributed in-house. Rather than creating a new application, simply add to the form a sticker, a check mark, a highlighted portion, or something that will be easy for the staff to recognize when registering new users.

## Library Use

### VISITORS TO THE LIBRARY

If your outreach records are detailed enough to include zip codes, or your library service area is clearly defined so that you know which library is most visited by a certain school, you can ask for the person counts for the specific library branch and evaluate these for any increase within a reasonable amount of time from the outreach visit. This type of statistic can be written as follows: "In the week/month/

number of days following an outreach visit to $X$ School, the number of visitors to the $X$ Library increased/decreased by $X$ number of visitors." This will give library administration a better idea of the immediate effect of outreach on visits to the library.

ONLINE VISITORS

Perhaps your priority for this year is to reach out to students in grades three through six and inform them of the resources available at the library for homework assignments. You gave out brochures, stickers, pencils, or some other kind of library material with a specific web address on it (perhaps directing them to the homework-help section of your library's kids page) so they would know specifically where to go when the time comes for help. Use past numbers of both total hits and new users (if available) to that specific site and compare these numbers on the same schedule as previous evaluations. Like new library card issuance, if there was no other unusual activity by local library staff and the number of hits to this website increased, you can safely say that outreach increased the traffic on this web page.

If you love compiling and comparing statistics, and your web reporting tools allow for more specificity, such as hits on very specific resource links, you may choose to delineate the effects of outreach further by saying the usage of the "Live Homework Help" resource, or any other specific electronic resource, increased by $X$ percent after extensive outreach promoting this service.

## Compiling Statistics

Properly compiling and evaluating the statistics you have is imperative. Automatic web-based database and statistics programs will save your staff not only time but also confusion in the compilation process. If you work with a library district large enough to afford a statistics software program or a person whose main job it is to compile statistics, you are quite lucky. Count your blessings and skip the rest of this chapter. If you are like the majority of library districts, which don't have that luxury, read on.

If it is part of your job to not only create, disseminate, and collect evaluations but also to compile the results of that information, you need to devote uninterrupted time to this task. You must pay attention to every detail, including what is not being evaluated. Data entry of the responses from surveys can be done by any staff member as long as he or she has been trained in how the software you will be using works and where exactly the information is entered. Simple spreadsheet and database programs can be used for this. A second person may want to check the hard copies of evaluations against the inputted numbers to ensure an accurate count. To better organize your time spent with statistics, take the following steps.

> Choose a specific day each week or month to submit the statistics to management (or at least to complete them departmentally).

> Allow two to four hours of uninterrupted office time each month for data entry.

> Clearly name the file where the statistics are kept and be sure to have it backed up on a separate disk. This file should be accessible to all.

> Take the time to create a how-to manual for your department on keeping statistics. This should include all relevant and specific information.

> Use a three-ring binder to keep all hard copies in, organized by date or visited agency, as well as a printout of each newly revised statistics worksheet.

Keeping statistics from your evaluation forms and reviewing them completely allows you to create and implement immediate changes (if needed) to your program. Once the materials have been compiled, you may need to graph each item to have a visual example of the effects of your outreach. This can be easily done through the same spreadsheet or database program you use to keep the hard numbers.

## Total Program Evaluation

At the end of your program year, sit down with your staff and discuss each of the statistics that have been recorded. Many programs may have seemed successful for a month but suddenly lost steam, or vice versa. Talk about what could have happened, what can be done to make it better, and whether it is your collective opinion that this particular program should continue. Think critically when evaluating the program. At the end of a program year, however you define it internally, you will need to make a determination of continuation or discontinuation. Most librarians hesitate to discontinue programs until they are absolutely certain they did all they could to make it successful. The staff have had a year for continuous improvement and evaluation. If at the end of the program year the effort is not deemed a total success as measured in increased library use, large attendance numbers, and awesome external evaluations, then it may be time to take on another project. If the project was a huge success, then making drastic changes may hurt its continuing success.

*Chapter Eight*

# Successful Library Youth Outreach Programs

**P**rofessional journals are filled with fantastic ideas and boasts about successful programs. Too often the pilot effort ends when funding ends, even though the program may have been successful. Most library districts provide outreach to youth on a branch level, but fewer are those who have distinct coordinated efforts in reaching out to youth. Some of the more successful programs are explored here. This list is by no means an inclusive list of successful programs.

## Las Vegas-Clark County Library District (LVCCLD)

http://www.lvccld.org

The Las Vegas–Clark County Library District (LVCCLD), winner of the 2003 Gale/Library Journal's Library of the Year and 2004 John Cotton Dana Public Relations Award, offers the Web on Wheels (WOW) program. The WOW program began in 2001 through partial funding from a Library Services and Technology Act (LSTA) grant. The original WOW mission and service goals follow:

> The Las Vegas–Clark County Library District introduces Web on Wheels (WOW)! WOW is a new program providing FREE

> assemblies or website training for K–5 students in our commu-
> nity schools. Our interactive assemblies promote the library,
> the services we provide and on-line resources available through
> our website. At the time of our visit, each student will receive
> special incentives to use library resources.[1]

Original programming focused on using a mix of traditional (storytelling, puppetry) and nontraditional (PowerPoint presentations)
activities in assemblies geared toward grade-school children. Schools
and other child-focused agencies were contacted by WOW staff via
telephone.

In true professional fashion, the WOW program has changed to accommodate the needs presented by the transient Las Vegas community. Three years later, the WOW mission statement was expanded:

> Reaching out beyond the traditional public library setting, we
> inspire and guide the diverse youth of our community, as well
> as their caregivers and teachers, toward lifelong learning and
> self-knowledge by introducing them to the many resources,
> educational tools, and opportunities for personal enrichment
> available through the Las Vegas–Clark County Library
> District.[2]

Services have also expanded to reflect the revised mission statement (see box 8.1).

Although the current website does not reflect the range of services offered, marketing is done through direct contact with estab-
lished and new community agencies and via word of mouth. By con-
tinually evaluating services, soliciting input from serviced agencies
and its staff, and following an ongoing districtwide strategic-planning
initiative, the library will likely keep this program successful.

**Box 8.1**

| Web on Wheels<br>Areas of Outreach Services | |
|---|---|
| **TYPE OF SERVICE** | **ELEMENTS INCLUDED IN THIS SERVICE** |
| Elementary school assembly | This is an "edutainment" type of program which may feature puppets, storytelling, and audience partici-pation to explore age-appropriate literature. This program usually also includes a brief introduction to the LVCCLD web page and the "secret" WOW password. |
| Elementary school database training | For 4th and 5th grades, children are introduced to the LVCCLD web page and provided an introduction to appropriate databases, such as *America the Beautiful, Lands and Peoples, New Book of Popular Science, Kids InfoBits, Junior Reference Collection,* and our Live Homework Help feature. This material is presented via a "live" Internet connection when appro-priate, or using a PowerPoint pres-entation. |
| Elementary school parent nights, open house | An informational table is set up to highlight LVCCLD services and pro-grams. A PowerPoint loop high-lighting our "Virtual Library" and appropriate databases is pre-sented, and library card applica-tions are available. Other informa-tion may be provided as requested. This service targets parents of school-age children. |
| Middle school database training | Middle school students are intro-duced to the LVCCLD web page, and to the online databases via the Teen Zone. This material is presented via a "live" Internet |

(cont.)

**Box 8.1** (cont.)

| TYPE OF SERVICE | ELEMENTS INCLUDED IN THIS SERVICE |
|---|---|
| Middle school database training (cont.) | connection in the school's computer lab. Classes are hands-on, and temporary library cards are left at the school to provide database access so teachers can reinforce the material presented. This information is more detailed than the elementary school version. WOW targets 6th grade classes, but is happy to work with any grade level as our schedule allows. |
| Middle school parent nights | Similar to elementary school parent nights. |
| High school database training | Much more involved than database training for younger students; the audience is presented with detailed information on acquiring a library card online, using a PIN number to request materials, searching the library catalog, and extensive exploration of the online databases. This information is presented "live" whenever possible, and students have "hands-on" time to complete a brief quiz. Temporary cards are left at the school to provide teachers and students an opportunity to explore the databases and reinforce the material presented. Our target is 9th grade, but we are happy to work with any grade level. |
| High school parent nights | Similar to elementary school parent nights. |
| After-school programs | These include both the City of Las Vegas and Clark County Safekey and Track Break sites. Programs can include any combination of storytelling, general library information, and database training. |

| TYPE OF SERVICE | ELEMENTS INCLUDED IN THIS SERVICE |
|---|---|
| Summer programs | These include Kids Kamps, Camp Odyssey, and Teen Kamps affiliated with the City of Las Vegas and Clark County. |
| Back-to-school events | Informational booths at back-to-school fairs sponsored by the city or county, and information presented to CCSD teachers, and librarians, PTA Leadership Training, and anything related to children, teachers, and parents preparing for the new school year. |
| Parks and rec and leisure services events | Puppet shows, informational booths, and craft activities presented in connection with city and county events—including Folklife, movie nights, children's concerts. |
| Services to un-served and under-served areas | Storytimes, database training, and library service informational programs conducted in areas of the Las Vegas valley without convenient access to a physical library. |
| Child care literacy training | L.E.A.P. (Language Enrichment Activities for Preschoolers) programs presented for city, county, and state-wide child care licensing departments highlighting best practices in early childhood literacy. Storytime training. |
| Family literacy training | WOW staff is trained to present early childhood literacy programs for parents, enhanced storytimes which focus on early childhood literacy skills, and PACT Time; as part of a 4-component family literacy program. |

*(cont.)*

Box 8.1  (cont.)

| TYPE OF SERVICE | ELEMENTS INCLUDED IN THIS SERVICE |
|---|---|
| General community outreach | Primarily informational booths at community events. We will usually provide library district information and a craft activity for children if requested. |
| LVCCLD program support | Middle School Survival presentations, SRP support, and other district-wide programs supported by WOW staff. |
| Other | Any other outreach activities not covered elsewhere, including workshops for teachers and library staff. |

# Multnomah County Library (MCL)

http://www.multcolib.org

The Multnomah County Library has its renowned School Corps program. The following description comes from the library's website:

> The Multnomah County Library School Corps connects students and educators with the critical information resources of the public library. The goal of the School Corps is to increase the information literacy of students in Multnomah County by working in partnership with local schools.[3]

On its website, the School Corps offers a "Menu of Services" that covers a range of topics, from using the library's electronic resources to the effect of censorship on children (see box 8.2). The menu includes the name of the service, intended audience by grade, minimum amount of time required, and any special equipment needs. Each of the programs is free of charge and can be scheduled via the e-mail contact listed on the page or via the telephone listed. There is a distinct service area, which is defined in the "Service Area" section of the website.

The "Menu of Services" is categorized into three sections: "Electronic Resources," "Curriculum Support," and "Your Public Library."[4]

Box 8.2

# Multnomah County Library
## School corps

### MENU OF SERVICES

#### *Electronic Resources*

*Library Catalog (grades 3–12, adult)*: Covers basic title, author and subject searches in the library's computerized catalog (either the text or Web version). Older students or educators can learn to use more advanced functions such as limiting, sorting and creating booklists. An Internet connection is required. 20-minute minimum.

*The Multnomah County Library of Websites (grades 3–12, adult)*: A survey of the library's websites appropriate for your audience. May include the KidsPage, the Homework Center, or the Outernet (for teens). An Internet connection is required. 10-minute minimum (per site).

*Library Databases Available from School or Home (grades 4–12, adult)*: The library provides access to many databases useful to teachers and students. This training can include Magazines Online, The Oregonian database, Grolier Online Encyclopedia, Electric Library, Facts on File, Biographies Plus, Opposing Viewpoints Resource Center, Oregon Career Information System, or the Literature Resource Center. An Internet connection is required. Students will need their Multnomah County Library cards to access the databases. 30-minute minimum.

*Introduction to Search Engines and How to Evaluate Websites (grades 6–12, adult)*: Covers basic Web searching and site evaluation skills, with a focus on the sites found in the library's Web directories. An Internet connection is required. 40-minute minimum.

*Live Homework Help (grades 4–12, adult)*: Learn how to access this program, which connects students one-on-one to qualified tutors online. Students will need their Multnomah County Library cards to use Live Homework Help. An Internet connection is required. 15-minute minimum.

*Think Before You Click (grades 4–12)*: This presentation about Internet safety and etiquette covers topics such as online privacy, advertising, spam, viruses, false information, and appropriate online behavior. Computer lab preferred. 45-minute minimum.

#### *Curriculum Support*

*Bucket of Books (grades K–12)*: These tubs contain 24–30 books on a topic plus a teacher's guide with an annotated list of age-appropriate websites, a pathfinder for doing research on the topic at Multnomah County Library, and instructions on how to obtain additional copies of the books.

*(cont.)*

**Box 8.2**  (cont.)

*Customized booklist (grades K–12):* If we don't have a Bucket of Books on your topic, check our booklist website, which has copies of our most popular booklists and instructions on how to create your own Bucket of Books using the lists. If your topic is not listed on the booklist site, we can create a customized booklist on a subject for your audience and send one copy of each book on the list to a nearby library for you to check out. Requires a three-week lead time.

*Customized webliography (grades K–12):* Let us create an annotated list of websites on a subject for your audience. Check the Homework Center to see if the library has already collected and annotated websites on your topic.

*Customized pathfinder (grades 3–12):* Will your students be visiting the Multnomah County Library to do research? We can create a guide to starting public library research on a topic for your students.

**Your Public Library**

*Check This Place Out! (grades K–4):* Answers basic questions about public libraries, including: What is a library? How do I get a library card? Requires an electrical outlet. 15-minute minimum.

*Great Authors and Illustrators (grades K–1, 2–3, and 4–5):* A look at some of the authors and illustrators of the books that young people like best, and how to find more about them on the Web. Requires an electrical outlet. 30-minute minimum.

*Feasting on Forbidden Fruit (grades 4–7 and 8–12):* How does censorship affect children and teens? Presentation includes an overview of censorship issues in the U.S., a PowerPoint presentation on challenged books, and a chance for students to review banned and challenged picture books. Requires an electrical outlet. One-hour minimum.

*Customized Booktalks (all ages):* Encourage your students to read! We can present booktalks on hot new titles, current award winners or award nominees.

From the School Corps website, there are services available to educators without even leaving your computer. Lists of staff-created book lists, online "Assignment Alert" forms, and information on "Educator Library Cards" are available at any time from any place. Web-based evaluation forms are available for both students and teachers and on specific services, such as training, presentation, or "Biblio/Weblio" services. These forms can be filled out completely online and upon completion are immediately sent to the appropriate administrator.

# Hennepin County Library (HCL)

http://www.hclib.org

Although youth outreach does not have a special place on the Hennepin County Library website, it is clear that outreach in general is a large focus of the library district. Their outreach mission statement makes that clear:

> The Hennepin County Library provides materials and services to meet the information and recreation needs of persons whose access to library services and materials is limited. These services, usually referred to as Outreach Services, are provided based on sensory, mental, physical, health, or behavioral conditions, or lack of transportation.[5]

Two of the more popular outreach efforts available are the Read Team and Great Transitions.

## Read Team

The goal of the Read Team outreach effort is to "enhance children's success in learning to read and reading to learn." Partnerships were created with three local school districts, and a specific timeline delineated by grade level is in place. Book bags are provided to all program participants. Presentations are given in schools and at parent and community meetings. The Read Team creates and distributes its own parent newsletters.[6]

## Great Transitions

The goal of the Great Transitions outreach effort is "to engage young people involved in the juvenile corrections system with the library and its array of resources and services in order to help them become avid readers and competent information seekers." [7] Great Transitions shows adjudicated youth how the library can help as they struggle, learn to change, and ultimately achieve. With its specific focus, statistics can be easily kept and evaluated. The Hennepin County Library brings library services to the corrections system, including booktalks and formal programming.

Both of these programs directly target youth as the outreach focus. The library also offers a "Toolbox for Teachers" via its website (http://www.hclib.org/ToolboxForTeachers/) (see figure 8.1).

On this site, teachers of all grades have access to important library information including sections on "Library Cards for Teachers and Students," "Classroom Workshops," and "School Visits to the Library." This inclusive site incorporates some of the most frequently requested services and products at the Hennepin County Library.

**HENNEPIN COUNTY Library** # *Toolbox for Teachers*

**www.hclib.org**

**Library Cards for Teachers & Students**
Use a library card to access Hennepin County Library's resources from home or school! Find out how to obtain a *free* Individual or Organization library card.

**Classroom Resources**
Integrate Hennepin County Library's online resources into your classroom curriculum. You'll find subject guides, tips on evaluating Web sites, online tutorials, and more.

**Classroom Workshops**
Hennepin County librarians will visit your classroom to help teach about online research in specific subject areas. Each workshop includes a consultation with a Hennepin County librarian beforehand, handouts for students, and advance library card registration when requested.

**Professional Development**
Schedule a free workshop for teachers at your school for a general introduction to TeenLinks, the library's online catalog, databases and other online reference tools. Each training includes a consultation with a Hennepin County librarian, handouts for students, and additional curricular resources.

**Professional Resources**
Hennepin County Library offers links to Web resources on Education such as ERIC and to subscription databases, such as Academic Search Premier and Professional Collection.

**School Visits to the Library**
Would you like to bring your students to a Hennepin County Library location? Find out how to schedule a visit.

Library Catalog

Library Home

TeenLinks

KidLinks

Featured Resources:

Web Design Contest

National History Day resources

Toolbox for Teachers was created by Hennepin County Library's *SWIFT* (Student/Web Instruction For Teachers) Project. For more information, please contact Cyndi Webster.

**Figure 8.1**

# Public Library of Charlotte and Mecklenburg County (PLCMC)

http://www.plcmc.org

Frequently recognized for its implementation of the authoritative StoryPlace (http://www.storyplace.org/), the Public Library of Charlotte and Mecklenburg County is active in many outreach efforts to children. The goals of its Youth Services Department include the following:

> Help young children develop the skills necessary
> to become readers
>
> Encourage youth to remain readers
>
> Empower youth to be independent doers and thinkers
>
> Impact family reading habits
>
> Promote the appreciation of quality literature
>
> Encourage youth to use the library as support for
> life-long learning[8]

Some of the programs available through the library follow.

## Storytimes to Go!

Storytimes to Go! is a program for preschool child-care providers that offers kits of story-time materials for use with children ages two to four.

## Connections That Count/Conexiones Que Cuentan

To address school readiness of Hispanic children, the Public Library of Charlotte and Mecklenburg County implemented Connections That Count/Conexiones Que Cuentan. The mission of this project is to prepare children from birth to age three for school by providing literacy training for families and encouraging the formation of "neighborhood teachers" for the children of their communities.

## The Westside Storytellers

The Westside Storytellers program offers early intervention preliteracy training to adults in child-care facilities, home-care providers, local four-year-old preschool programs, parenting programs, and other community-based agencies via customized workshops linking library resources to curriculum, providing book deposit collections, and offering parent-teacher resources, in addition to modeling storytelling skills.

## Continue the Contact . . . Read Together

Continue the Contact . . . Read Together is a partnership between the library and the Youth and Family Services Division of the Mecklenburg County Department of Social Services. The project works by providing backpacks filled with both educational and fun items to children entering foster care. The children are encouraged to carry the backpacks as well as some of the books and other activities they received with the backpacks on each visit with their birth families. Reading journals and parent journals are provided to help promote reading together and strengthen the lines of communication between birth and foster families.[9]

■ ■ ■ ■ ■

Although each of these programs has differences, similarities among successful outreach programs include dedicated staff, organized efforts, and constant evaluation and program response. Your library, too, can be as successful. If you have any questions about the programs listed here, you are encouraged to contact the library. All of these library districts have been very accommodating in sharing their program information.

### NOTES

1. Las Vegas–Clark County Library District, Web on Wheels. Available from http://www.lvccld.org/wow/wow_children.htm.
2. Evelyn Walkowicz, Youth Outreach Librarian, Las Vegas–Clark County Library District, e-mail message to author, August 25, 2004.
3. Multnomah County Library, School Corps, "Mission." Available from http://www.multcolib.org/schoolcorps/mission.html.
4. Multnomah County Library, School Corps, "Menu of Services." Available from http://www.multcolib.org/schoolcorps/menu.html.
5. Patrick Jones, Outreach Services Manager, Hennepin County Library, e-mail message to author, August 27, 2004.
6. Ibid.
7. Ibid.
8. Public Library of Charlotte and Mecklenburg County, Youth Services. Available from http://www.plcmc.org/youth/default.htm.
9. Ibid.

# Chapter Nine

# Putting It All Together

**M**arketing is more than just promotion and public relations. It involves specific planning, strategic implementation, and constant evaluation. Outreach encompasses all of the qualities of marketing, for each element of every program strives to meet certain goals, reach targeted audiences, and disseminate information. Library youth outreach efforts must mimic the same accountability as marketing. To effectively implement a successful plan, whether marketing or outreach or both, the program must have clearly defined budgetary and staffing objectives, a detailed plan of action, and constant support. Using materials and programs already created will seemingly lessen the planning process but not reduce the anticipated outcome. It all starts with an IDEA.

**I** = Identify need

**D** = Design programs

**E** = Evaluate service

**A** = Add new programs

## Identify Need

As with developing a marketing plan, when you begin a youth outreach initiative, you must define the need. This need should be defined through your market analysis, through looking at your library district's strategic planning goals, and through community input. After conducting your market analysis of existing agencies and their services, think critically about how the library can either enhance an existing program or fill an obvious void in literacy or information programming. For example, if the local Boys and Girls Club offers supervised after-school programs for students in grades K–8 but generally offers only physical activities such as sports, game rooms, and other nonintellectual diversions, look at what else the kids need that they cannot get from this agency because of the agency's budgetary or staffing restraints. Every child who attends school, no matter if it is public or private, at home or online, will have homework. To complete their homework, students not only need a quiet place to work but also need such resources as reference books, supplies, and maybe just some solid advice. Libraries can use ingenious ideas—such as providing a librarian armed with books or a laptop using a wireless connection—to encourage students to complete their homework. Many public librarians are finally embracing the idea that for a child to become a *lifelong* learner, he or she first needs to be a *learner*. Libraries should never replace schools as the main educational resource, yet we can offer students empowerment when completing their homework assignments. Identifying a specific need helps you to better articulate and design programs to meet the need.

## Design Programs

With your need clearly articulated, you can begin designing programs. The design phase incorporates planning for, securing, and using dedicated funds. As previously discussed, having a specific program budget will help you to design programs that are affordable. Your staff will ensure programs are designed to be useful. Creating programs that are both affordable and useful is imperative, especially when these programs will be delivered off-site at locations that will change daily.

When designing your programs, the identified need should be a priority. The need may be too abstract to present straightforwardly or not exciting enough to keep the attention of children. Use your creativity in presentations. Incorporate puppets and storytelling and appeal to the children's sense of urgency to get your message across. Programs can be as simple as handing out library cards and explaining responsibility to large-scale productions with music and puppets.

## Evaluate Service

Make it a priority to continuously evaluate your programs. With constant evaluation, both internal and external, you will be able to best amend, enhance, or even discontinue certain efforts. Do not hesitate to stop offering a program. Discontinuing a program should only be done, however, when all measures point to the program's ineffectiveness. Don't think of this as a failure; think of it as an opportunity to refocus your efforts on successful programs. In your evaluations, be sure to consider all factors that may have contributed to a successful program. These factors are sure to include library staff not directly involved in the external dissemination of information. All staff should be evaluated to learn their thoughts on the effectiveness of the program.

## Add New Programs

Once your existing program is well defined, clearly outlined, and presented with ease and authoritativeness, and that program shows promise through your evaluations, continue to add new programs, new sites, and new presentations. Add programs slowly to ensure enough time for evaluations. As programs are added, new goals and objectives will need to be added to the marketing plan. Your marketing plan is a dynamic document and should change as often as the identified need changes.

After developing your IDEA, ensure that your outreach staff members have some basic knowledge of outreach. Author and consultant Patrick Jones (http://www.connectingya.com) drafted a "Core Competencies of Outreach" and detailed eight distinct areas of competency that are needed to make outreach successful. While these competencies were not specifically created for youth outreach staff or services, each of the areas mentioned is easily applied to youth services.

## AREA I
# Leadership and Professionalism

The librarian will be able to:

> Demonstrate a non-judgmental attitude toward underserved populations, and demonstrate an understanding of and a respect for diversity in cultural values.

> Plan for personal and professional growth and career development through active participation in professional associations and continuing education.

> Develop and demonstrate a strong commitment to the right of underserved populations to have physical and intellectual access to information that is consistent with the American Library Association's Library Bill of Rights.

> Encourage underserved populations to become lifelong library users by helping them to discover what libraries have to offer and how to use libraries.

## AREA II
# Knowledge of Client Group

The librarian will be able to:

> Identify the needs of discrete groups of underserved populations and design and implement programs and build collections appropriate to their needs.

> Identify information resources, including community members and organizations, which can provide the library with knowledge of the information needs of underserved populations.

> Understand the obstacles to library use faced by underserved populations.

## AREA III
# Communication

The librarian will be able to:

> Demonstrate effective interpersonal relations with under-served populations, administrators, other professionals who work with underserved populations, and the community at large.

> Be able to speak effectively about library services in front of large and small groups, in formal and informal settings, and in settings outside of the library.

> Be able to network effectively among, and develop professional relationships with, members of the business, human services, and other community members.

## AREA IV
# Administration

The librarian will be able to:

> Develop a strategic plan for library service to underserved populations, which includes formulating goals, objectives, and methods of evaluation for an outreach program based on determined needs.

> Design and conduct a community analysis and needs assessment.

> Design, implement, and evaluate an ongoing public relations and report program directed toward underserved populations, administrators, boards, staff, other agencies, and the community at large.

> Identify and cooperate with other information agencies in networking arrangements to expand access to information for underserved populations.

> Develop physical facilities which contribute to the achievement of outreach program goals.

## AREA V
# Knowledge of Materials

The librarian will be able to:

Formulate collection development and selection policies for materials of interest to underserved populations, consistent with the parent institutions' policies.

Using a broad range of selection sources, develop a collection of materials for underserved populations that includes all appropriate formats.

Incorporate new and improved technology (e.g., computers and software, digitized information, video, the Internet, and the World Wide Web) into outreach services.

Maintain awareness of ongoing technological advances and a minimum level of expertise with electronic resources.

## AREA VI
# Access to Information

The librarian will be able to:

Organize collections to guarantee easy and equitable access to information for underserved populations.

Create an environment which attracts and invites underserved populations to use the collection.

Develop tools which provide access to information not readily available (e.g., community resources, special collections, and links to appropriate and useful websites).

Create and disseminate promotional materials that will ease access to collections and motivate their use in appropriate languages and formats.

## AREA VII
# Personal competencies

The librarian will be able to:

Demonstrate effective time management techniques.

Demonstrate effective personal characteristics such as patience, persistence, sense of humor, and tolerance when interacting with underserved populations and community partners.

Think creatively to identify solutions to remove obstacles faced by underserved populations.

## AREA VIII
## Services

The librarian will be able to:

Provide a variety of information services to meet the diverse needs of underserved populations.

Instruct underserved populations in the basic information gathering and research skills. These should include the skills necessary to use and evaluate electronic information sources, and to insure current and future information literacy.

Encourage underserved populations in the use of all types of materials for their personal growth and enjoyment.

Design, implement, and evaluate specific programs and activities (both in the library and in the community) for underserved populations, based on their needs and interests.

Involve underserved populations in planning and implementing services and programs for their age group.[1]

Consider these competencies when creating your outreach plan, hiring your staff, and providing staff training.

## Conclusion

Marketing and outreach are not separate. They are directly related to one another. The more marketing you do, the more results you will have. Outreach follows this same premise. Create a marketing plan for your library, or scrutinize the one you have in place now. Be sure that marketing and outreach goals and objectives are defined. When performing a market analysis, no matter how formal, be sure to do it objectively. Leave any organizational history out of this plan. This is your opportunity not only to begin to attract new users but it is also a perfect time to redefine the library's image. When preparing your marketing materials, especially those that are targeted at children, be aware of the developmental and social needs of children. Use graphics rather than text when possible and keep the language simple. Prominently display the library logo on all materials that are distributed about the library. Novelty marketing items should be useful and necessary items for students and children.

Outreach begins in-house. Look at what you do now and ask yourself how you can do it better and where. Library programs can be library programs regardless of where they are held. Use your marketing plan when determining outreach sites and create a detailed list of agencies. Don't forget to include your library website in your plan. Online services are also outreach, technically, as they are not in any physical library space. Use your website to your advantage with children. Offer traditional programs online and ask children for their input so you are able to best evaluate these programs. Keep track of all of your outreach, but be sure to keep the same information on each of the presentations. Have a standard list of queries ready before you begin soliciting external information. Read through, scrutinize, and capitalize on all information from external sites. Review, reevaluate, and redesign your outreach and marketing efforts as often as needed. Look to existing successful libraries for mentorship. Most libraries are happy to share not only their successes but also their failures.

Children in your communities need you to advocate for their needs, but to be effective, you have to know what those needs are. Outreach to children takes a special desire to work with children; an understanding of library services, policies, and procedures; and an extensive amount of energy. While outreach can be the most exhausting work in libraries, it can also be the most rewarding. Knowing that you did not wait for the kids to come to you but went out and brought them the library's services is an intrinsic reward that really cannot be measured.

NOTE

1. Patrick Jones. *Core Competencies of Outreach.* 2003. Available from
   http://www.connectingya.com.

*Appendix A*

# Sample
# Outreach
# Programs

**A**s you have read, outreach and marketing can be as simple or elaborate as you can imagine and support. Youth services staff pride themselves on creating well-attended programs, but rarely are the programs repeated. Outreach is an opportune time to use existing programs and bring them to the community. The following are examples of simple and elaborate outreach programs.

## Simple Outreach Programs

In chapter 2, marketing materials were discussed; hopefully, your library has at least one of these informational items. Simple outreach programs may use existing promotional materials as a program.

### Library Maps

Library location maps have more uses than just helping users find the libraries. In many elementary school curricula across the country, children are taught all they might need to know about maps, including how to locate something on a map, using a key, and giving directions from a map. Distribute your library maps with an attached worksheet detailing which curricula your materials will meet. Box A.1 is a sample teacher's guide to distribute with maps.

# Using the Library Map in Your Classroom
## TEACHER'S GUIDE

The following activity will meet specific curricula criteria. [List specific information here.]

1. Distribute one library map to each student. Review the parts of a map:

   ■ Key
   ■ Legend
   ■ Directions

2. Using the maps handed out to each student, have students mark your school location on the map.

3. Pick a library to travel to and have the students mark the best way to get there on the map.

4. Once students have created their paths, ask students to write out directions to the library. This can be given as homework with help from parents.

5. Students should return the written portion to you and keep the library map for themselves.

### Books on Maps

[List books available in your library district, complete with title, author, and call number.]

### Electronic Resources

To access library resources through the library website [list web address], students will need to have a valid library card. [List all electronic resources available remotely that feature age-appropriate maps and atlases. Many electronic encyclopedias include detailed atlases.]

## Library Card Applications

A library card application can be a great self-invitation to visit the classroom. It can be easily incorporated into the classroom as either a handwriting or life-skills tool. Distribute library card applications with an attached teacher's guide detailing this information and a sample outline for use (see box A.2).

## Theme-Based Story Kits

Most public libraries offer story times to go in a bag, box, or in some way packaged for easy transport and use by external educators. If these kits are listed in the library's catalog, they are often difficult to locate or to understand what they are. If kits are not advertised, it is likely they are rarely used. Your kit should contain a list of curricular needs that it meets. Teachers find the list very useful when being accountable for their class lessons. Make use of these small deposit collections. Don't just tell teachers about them; visit schools with one in hand to display and a brochure or printout on how to find and request them in the library. Yes, sell your kits. Don't have time for door-to-door sales? Use the kits yourself when providing outreach services to child-focused community agencies, and when your program is over, let the educators know they too have access to these kits. This in itself is fantastic promotion. If the kit is not appealing to you, then it probably won't be appealing to educators. Make necessary changes to materials included in the kit so they are more desirable.

■ ■ ■ ■ ■

Simple programs use what you already have, what is readily available, and those skills that you have perfected. For simple programs, you may choose to use one of your popular in-house class-visit story times and simply deliver it in schools. Programs using library informational materials, such as the ones above, seek to not only create awareness of the library but to get something library related into the hands of children. Along with all of your simple story times, distribute a resource list that the agency can refer to in your absence.

# Using the Library Card Application in Your Classroom

## TEACHER'S GUIDE

The following activity will meet specific curricula criteria. [List specific information here.]

1. Students will learn how to fill out a form, practice their handwriting skills, and learn about responsibility.
2. Distribute library card applications to each of your students.
3. Spend time reviewing each of the areas to be filled in.
4. For the application to be complete, students will need to have the form signed by a parent or guardian.
5. Collect all of the signed applications and drop them off at your closest library. Please be sure to speak with the youth services staff about scheduling a time for a staff member to come to your class with the actual cards.
6. The library staff member who visits your classroom will discuss library card responsibilities and demonstrate some of the information and programs available at the library. Once the cards are distributed to students, they will be required to sign their names on the back.

### Library-Related Books for Reading Aloud

[List library-related books available from your library, complete with title, author, and call number.]

# Elaborate Outreach Programs

All libraries create special, big, elaborate programs for children at least once a year, most commonly during the summer reading program. Programs are planned to be reflective of the library as well as to accommodate large crowds. As with your simple outreach programs, elaborate programs can easily be transported to an outside site.

## Curriculum-Based Programs

### SCIENCE FAIR

Almost every student at some point or another is expected to participate in a school science fair. These students descend upon our libraries in droves looking for the perfect project, many coming the day before the project is due. We know this assignment is coming, and we have begun to prepare our staff and branches by having displays of science-project resources pulled out from the general collection to make the customer's visit more efficient. Some libraries have a series of programs specifically about science projects to offer personal attention and science-fair help to those who attend (see box A.3 for a sample science project assembly). Create a list of useful resources for completing science projects and be sure to include all electronic resources that are available remotely. When delivering this program, show the students how to do a science project. Actually perform one. Take them through a quick tour of the electronic resources available. Show them some books. Read science-related stories.

### PRESIDENTS

At some point in their elementary school career, students will be asked to read and write about a president. Libraries are well equipped to handle the questions with the numerous book series available for each president and the presidential reference encyclopedias and dictionaries. Many districts have thorough electronic resources that will effectively aid in meeting specific presidential biography needs. Students commonly enter the library and do not know where to start. Using the sample assembly in box A.4, go to their classrooms, lunchrooms, and schools and give them a head start on their research.

# Science-Project Assembly

## Props and Equipment Needed

- Computer and projector
- Live Internet connection
- Lab coat for presenter and any items required to perform the science experiment
- Books for display

## Materials to Present

The presenter should be dressed as a scientist. Use a lab coat and have pictures or props of beakers, microscopes, etc., to enhance the set. If two presenters are available, perform a rendition of "Take Me Out to the Ball Game" from Dee Anderson's *Amazingly Easy Puppet Plays: 42 New Scripts for One-Person Puppetry* (Chicago: American Library Association, 1996) .

### DEMONSTRATE A SIMPLE SCIENCE EXPERIMENT

Demonstrate a simple experiment for the students; something that shows science in action should be sufficient. The experiment should also be something that is easy to transport, set up, and clean up. Optical illusions are always a favorite. The illusion can be placed on the computer and projected to a larger size so all can see.

### LOCATE SCIENCE EXPERIMENTS

Demonstrate science-related databases using the live Internet connection. Project the home page to a larger size so all can see.

Demonstrate searching the library catalog, including specific terms to use when looking for science projects.

### WHAT BOOKS DO YOU HAVE?

Have a small display of books that are available at the library.

## Handouts

- Library card applications
- Map to the library
- Science Fair Pathfinder (for easily finding information on science projects)

The program will take about twenty-five to thirty minutes without questions from the audience.

# Presidential Assembly

## *Props and Equipment Needed*

- Library seal, or logo, to be displayed in front of the podium or table where the outreach staff will be speaking.
- Computer and projector
- Live Internet connection
- Books for display

## *Materials to Present*

The presenter will act as a president by being nicely dressed and addressing the students as a president would address audience members at a speaking engagement. Begin by engaging students in a casual conversation while testing them on current presidential knowledge. Ask questions that require only a one- or two-word answer.

### READ ALOUD

A good book to read selections from is Judith St. George's *So You Want to Be President?* (New York: Philomel, 2000).

### LOCATE PRESIDENTIAL INFORMATION

Demonstrate and describe how to use specific databases from home Demonstrate the library catalog, including specific search terms to use when looking for presidents.

### WHAT BOOKS DO YOU HAVE?

Have a small display of various types of presidential books available at the library.

## *Handouts*

- Library card applications
- Map to the library
- Presidential Pathfinder (for easily finding information on presidents)

The program will take about twenty-five to thirty minutes without questions from the audience.

The presidential program can be easily modified to demonstrate searching for general biographies.

■ ■ ■ ■ ■

Because most of the elaborate programs feature small book displays, you may choose to offer remote checkout of those books if the students have library cards. Remote checkout availability will vary by district, so know your district policy before offering this. Should you be able to offer this feature, it can be treated as a prize, and the student who checks out the book can be designated a winner. You may even be able to offer remote checkout to the teachers for use in their classrooms, provided they have their library cards handy.

*Appendix B*

# Additional Reading

## General Library Marketing

de Saez, Eileen Elliott. *Marketing Concepts for Libraries and Information Services*. 2d ed. London: Library Association, 2002.

Fleck, Jim. *The Library Story: How to Market Your Library through Story*. Columbia City, IN: FLC, 1994.

Hart, Keith. *Putting Marketing Ideas into Action*. Successful LIS Professional Series 45004000. London: Library Association, 1998.

Karp, Rashelle S. *Powerful Public Relations: A How-to Guide for Libraries*. Chicago: American Library Association, 2002.

Kotler, Philip. *Strategic Marketing for Nonprofit Organizations*. 4th ed. Englewood Cliffs, NJ: Prentice Hall, 1991.

Owens, Irene. *Strategic Marketing in Library and Information Science*. Binghamton, NY: Haworth, 2003.

Seiss, Judith A. *The Visible Librarian: Asserting Your Value with Marketing and Advocacy*. Chicago: American Library Association, 2003.

Tenney, H. Baird. *Marketing and Libraries Do Mix: A Handbook for Libraries and Information Centers*. Columbus, Ohio: State Library of Ohio, 1993.

Wallace, Linda K. *Libraries, Mission and Marketing: Writing Mission Statements That Work*. Chicago: American Library Association, 2004.

Walters, Suzanne. *Library Marketing That Works!* New York: Neal-Schuman, 2004.

Weingand, Darlene. *Future-Driven Library Marketing*. Chicago: American Library Association, 1998.

Wolfe, Lisa A. *Library Public Relations, Promotions, and Communications: A How-to-Do-It Manual*. How-to-Do-It Manuals for Libraries, 75. New York: Neal-Schuman, 2003.

## Program-Specific Marketing

Barclay, Donald A. *Teaching and Marketing Electronic Information Literacy Programs: A How-to-Do-It Manual for Librarians*. How-to-Do-It Manuals for Libraries, 124. New York: Neal-Schuman, 2003.

Barker, Sharon L., and Karen L. Wallace, eds. *The Responsive Public Library: How to Develop and Market a Winning Collection*. 2d ed. Englewood, CO: Libraries Unlimited, 2002.

Jones, Patrick. *Running a Successful Library Card Campaign*. New York: Neal-Schuman, 2002.

Trotta, Marcia. *Managing Library Outreach Programs: A How-to-Do-It Manual for Librarians*. How-to-Do-It Manuals for Libraries. New York: Neal-Schuman, 1993.

## Marketing to Children

Acuff, Daniel. *What Kids Buy and Why: The Psychology of Marketing to Kids*. New York: Free Press, 1998.

Campbell, Kim, and Kent Davis-Packard. "How Ads Get Kids to Say I Want It!" *Christian Science Monitor*, September 18, 2000.

Del Vecchio, Gene. *Creating Ever-Cool: A Marketer's Guide to a Kid's Heart*. Gretna, LA: Pelican, 1997.

Lindstrom, Martin. *BRANDchild: Insights into the Minds of Today's Global Kids: Understanding Their Relationship with Brands*. Sterling, VA: Kogan Page, 2003.

Linn, Susan. *Consuming Kids: The Hostile Takeover of Childhood*. New York: New Press, 2004.

McNeal, James. *The Kids Market: Myths and Realities*. Ithaca, NY: Paramount Market, 1999.

Sutherland, Anne, and Beth Thompson. *Kidfluence: The Marketer's Guide to Understanding and Reaching Generation Y—Kids, Tweens, and Teens*. New York: McGraw-Hill, 2003.

# SELECTED BIBLIOGRAPHY

"Brand Aware." *Children's Business*, June 2000.

Jones, Patrick. *Core Competencies of Outreach*. 2003. Available from http://www.connectingya.com.

Las Vegas–Clark County Library District. Web on Wheels. Available from http://www.lvccld.org/wow/wow_children.htm.

McNeal, James. *The Kids Market: Myths and Realities* (Ithaca, NY: Paramount Market, 1999).

———. "Tapping the Three Kids' Markets." *American Demographics*, April 1998.

McNeal, James, and Chyon-Hwa Yeh. "Born to Shop." *American Demographics*, June 1993.

Merriam-Webster's Online Dictionary. Available from http://www.m-w.com.

Multnomah County Library. School Corps, "Menu of Services." Available from http://www.multcolib.org/schoolcorps/menu.html.

———. School Corps, "Mission." Available from http://www.multcolib.org/schoolcorps/mission.html.

National Center for Educational Statistics. Library Statistics Program. "Programs for Adults in Public Library Outlets." Available from http://nces.ed.gov/pubs2003/2003010.pdf.

———. "Public Libraries in the United States: Fiscal Year 2001." Available from http://nces.ed.gov/pubs2003/2003399.pdf.

Nestle, Marion, and Margo Wootan. "Spending on Marketing to Kids Up $5 Billion in Last Decade." *Food Institute Report*, April 15, 2002.

Public Library of Charlotte and Mecklenburg County. StoryPlace. Available from http://www.storyplace.org/about.asp.

———. Youth Services. Available from http://www.plcmc.org/youth/default.htm.

Weingand, Darlene. *Marketing/Planning Library and Information Services*, 2d ed. (Littleton, CO: Libraries Unlimited, 1999).

# INDEX

**Angela B. Pfeil** is a virtual reference librarian for Tutor.com's Librarians by Request and owner of Pfeil Consulting (http://www.pfeilconsulting.com). With a passion for serving underserved youth populations, she has worked as a youth services librarian, outreach librarian, and literacy trainer in the Las Vegas, Nevada, area for more than seven years. Pfeil earned her MLS degree at the State University of New York at Buffalo and her MA in Educational Counseling at the University of Phoenix. She can be contacted at angela@pfeilconsulting.com.